THE WINES OF FRANCE

Cyril Ray, born 1908, was a scholar both of Manchester
Grammar School and of Jesus College, Oxford. He has been
a war correspondent, a foreign correspondent, and a
UNESCO special commissioner in various European and
African countries. He has been 'Atticus' of the *Sunday Times*,
assistant editor of the *Spectator*, and author of military histor-
ies, but is best-known as a writer on wine.

In 1965, Cyril Ray received the Wine and Food Society's
first André Simon Award for his services to gastronomic
literature and especially for his editorship of the then annual
anthology, *The Compleat Imbiber*. In 1967, with the publication of *The Wines of Italy* (in Penguin Books), which was
translated into Italian, he became the first Englishman to be
awarded Italy's similar prize, the Bologna Trophy.

Founder, now President, of the Circle of Wine Writers,
Cyril Ray has been honoured by the Italian and the French
governments for his contributions to the literature of wine:
he is a Cavaliere dell' Ordine al Merito della Repubblica
Italiana and a Chevalier du Mérite Agricole.

He recently collaborated with his wife, Elizabeth – cookery
correspondent of the *Observer* and editor of *The Best of Eliza
Acton*, which is in Penguin Books – in a light-hearted work
of pooled knowledge and experience, *Wine with Food*. Cyril
Ray's latest book is *The Wines of Germany*, published by Allen
Lane in 1977.

On wine and kindred subjects

The Gourmet's Companion (edited with an introduction)
The Compleat Imbiber, Nos. 1–12 (edited)
The Wines of Italy
Morton Shand's *A Book of French Wines* (revised and edited)
In a Glass Lightly
Lafite: The Story of Château Lafite-Rothschild
Bollinger: The Story of a Champagne
Cognac
Mouton-Rothschild
Wine with Food (with Elizabeth Ray)
The Wines of Germany
The Complete Book of Spirits and Liqueurs

On other subjects

Scenes and Characters from Surtees (edited with an introduction)
From Algiers to Austria: The History of 78 Division
The Pageant of London
Merry England
Regiment of the Line: The Story of the Lancashire Fusiliers
Best Murder Stories (edited with an introduction)

THE
WINES
OF
FRANCE

*

CYRIL RAY

PENGUIN BOOKS

Penguin Books Ltd, Harmondsworth, Middlesex, England
Penguin Books, 625 Madison Avenue, New York, New York 10022, U.S.A.
Penguin Books Australia Ltd, Ringwood, Victoria, Australia
Penguin Books Canada Ltd, 2801 John Street, Markham, Ontario, Canada L3R 1B4
Penguin Books (N.Z.) Ltd, 182-190 Wairau Road, Auckland 10, New Zealand

—

First published by Allen Lane 1976
Published in Penguin Books 1978

—

Copyright © Cyril Ray, 1976
All rights reserved

—

Made and printed in Great Britain by
Richard Clay (The Chaucer Press) Ltd, Bungay, Suffolk
Set in Monotype Bembo

Contents

Maps

Introduction

A DOZEN years or so ago, I revised for Penguin Books the late Morton Shand's *A Book of French Wines*; it duly appeared in paperback for the first time, in 1964.

In 1974, Penguin Books asked me to bring it again up to date. I was flattered to be asked, but felt obliged to point out that the book had first been published in 1928, had been revised by its author for a new edition in 1960, and then further revised by myself in 1963.

It had become, I said, rather like a pair of boots that had been soled and heeled a couple of times, and now needed new uppers. What was wanted was a new pair altogether.

Not that Morton Shand's book is not itself still a minor classic. It will not only retain an honoured place on my shelves – as, I am sure, on those of other amateurs of wine – but will frequently be reached for. It is full of provocative ideas, felicitous turns of phrase, and apt quotations.

But it is no longer a practical guide to the wines of France.

There have been so many changes in methods of vine-growing and of wine-making, in French law and in British taste, in the economics of growing and the economics of drinking, that it is no longer possible to amend still further a book first written almost half a century ago.

What is more, Morton Shand wrote for a more leisurely age than ours – not that he thought that the nineteen-twenties were leisurely: he wrote of 'the strain and competitive haste of post-war life' breeding 'an impatience to enjoy', and of wine that had 'grown, and relentlessly went on growing, so much dearer that most families found less and less to spare for it'.

This when a *cru classé* claret of a good year cost five or six shillings a bottle, vintage port for laying down about the same, and a respectable *vin ordinaire* a shilling or so.

Now, when a first-growth claret, ready to drink – say the Cheval Blanc 1962 – costs more than £10 a bottle in a wine-merchant's shop, perhaps twice as much in a restaurant, and one is hard put to it to find sound *vins ordinaires* at less than a pound a bottle, most families are nevertheless finding not less and less but more and more money to spare: prices have risen steeply, consumption more steeply still.

But the pattern has altered: if there is more money to spare, it is for different wines. We look now not only to countries other than France but towards regions of France itself the wines of which never came to Britain in Morton Shand's time: VDQS wines (*vins délimités de qualité supérieure*), the status of which is explained in Chapter 1, have assumed a new importance, and the newly-created official category of *vins de pays* will also come to loom larger in our lives.

Another development that has dated Morton Shand's book is the widening of the British market for wines: when he first wrote, it was dons and country doctors, the Inns of Court and the West-End clubs, that set the tone for wine-lists and for books about wine. They were catered for by old-fashioned wine-merchants, themselves often leisured and scholarly. Now, it is not only these, but the young people on package tours whose parents before them had never been abroad in their lives, or had a bottle of wine on their tables; the house-wife in the supermarket; and all the rest of us.

On the whole, the dons and the doctors, the lawyers and the clubmen, were stay-at-homes. They read books about wine in their smoking-rooms or their studies or their senior common rooms, able not only to translate for themselves Morton Shand's quotations from Ronsard and Rabelais, Molière and Madame de Sévigné (it was typical of the times that the author expected them to), but to sink with deep sighs, as though into leather armchairs, into the embraces of Shand quoting Rabelais:

> Goustez à tasse pleine et canoniquement
> De ce laict purpurin, doulce revalascière,
> Qui résjouit le cœur et faict l'esprit libère:
> Dès l'aube à la vesprée, humez-le lentement

before going on:

Bordeaux, which was first belauded by Ausonius, has been called 'austere' and again *un gentleman par excellence, le vin d'une correction impeccable*. Maurice des Ombiaux defines it as a wine of perfect scansion and rhythm, evocative of the polished verse of Racine or La Fontaine. To compare the magnificent harmony of a fine Bordeaux to a flight of alexandrines is to pay it a doubtful compliment – outside of France at least – for the genius of no great wine is less emphatic, declamatory, or monotonous. Grandeur it has, and in high degree, but I find the 'scansion' of Bordeaux, if scansion there must be, ranges from the Horatian to the Miltonic, from the rippling lyrics of Herrick to the sway and surge of Swinburne in the infinite variety of its scope; the 'rhythm' of its incarnadine burden, the lilt of splendid majesty, never the din of rant drowning the creaking of the buskins. It is a wine of superb carriage, of gracious manners, but its charms, as its virtues, are wholly feminine. Bordeaux is a great lady, not a *Grand Seigneur*.

Nowadays, most of us travel more widely and read more narrowly – even in our own language, let alone the others. And Morton Shand's baroque manner of writing about wine, which he shared with Maurice Healy and Warner Allen, is as dead as Dada. The very name of Raymond Postgate's marvellously helpful little book, which first came out in 1951 (and is still, happily, in print) ushered in the new age of wine-writing. *The Plain Man's Guide to Wine* was written in plain English, and so must be any book about wine of the nineteen-seventies. The furthest flight of fancy that Raymond Postgate allowed himself was to observe that sauternes is a delightful wine, 'taken at the right time – which is after the main dish, with fruit or dessert – and in the right company, which is a plump, pretty and rather greedy young woman'. Compare and contrast, as the examiners say, with Morton Shand's literary dithyrambs.

Morton Shand wrote for the scholar in his armchair; now, in writing a Penguin book to replace his, one must write not only for the old-established customer of the old-established wine-merchant but for the shopper in the supermarket or the branch of a chain of brewery-owned shops, the family on a fortnight's holiday in France – a book not for the study but for the glove-compartment in a motor car.

So, although this little book is meant as a successor in the Penguin list of handbooks to Morton Shand's *A Book of French Wines*, it is modelled much more closely on my own Penguin, *The Wines of Italy*.

As in that little guide, after a sketch of the historical background, I take each wine-growing region of the country separately, introduce it briefly, and then list its wines, with a note on each. In the Italian book, written after the passing of the law of the Denominazioni di Origine Controllata, but before an official list was issued of the DOC wines, I listed all the wines the names of which I knew to be officially or even generally recognized, taking various Italian works on wines as check-lists. In this book, I list all wines entitled by French law to an *appellation contrôlée*, or to bear the seal denoting a *vin délimité de qualité supérieure*. My guide has been the list submitted by the French Ministry of Agriculture to the EEC in September 1973, with later additions and amendments, as issued up to May 1975, and I take the regions in the same order – approximately clockwise round the country.

The French law of AOC and VDQS is explained in Chapter 1 (pages 29–30).

It will be seen, then, that this is no attempt to relate the adventures of my soul among masterpieces, to use a quotation from Anatole France that Morton Shand permitted to escape.

My aim has been to give to the shopper in the supermarket, the older-fashioned wine-merchant's customer, the traveller in France, some idea of the general character of each region's wines, with rather more particular notes on those that are considered outstanding.

What, alas, I am unable to do is to provide a guide to those wines – even those French wines – sold widely now in supermarkets and high-street chain-wine-merchants under brand names. In France, such wines are also sold under brand names and by alcoholic strength – the stronger the wine the higher the price.

Such wines are often good of their kind, sometimes very good. They are almost always good value. But they do not have a local habitation and a name, and this book is about specific wines from specific regions of France.*

*It may be of help, though, to travellers in France to mention here that in February 1974 the French monthly, *50 Millions de Consommateurs*, published the findings of a committee consisting of analytical chemists, wine-tasters from the trade and members of the fraud squad, who had tasted forty bottles of red wine sold under brand names in supermarkets.

The brands chosen were the best-sellers out of a couple of hundred.

Such wines, they concluded, were all blends, each blend consisting usually of 60 to 90 per cent of wines from Languedoc-Roussillon (less frequently from the Loire or the Bordelais), 3 to 5 per cent of wines from the south that had been declassified because they were surplus to the VDQS quota, wine from hybrid grapes, not permitted to AOC and VDQS wines and, in certain cases, 5 to 10 per cent of Italian wine.

None was adulterated: they were genuinely *wine*.

'The tasters found some wines very pleasant to drink: Valcoop 11 degrees, Grap 11 degrees, Clairet and Fantonnet.' Differences in price reflected only alcoholic strength, not quality, and the best value for money seemed to be offered by Valcoop 10 degrees, La Tonnelle 11 degrees, and Taille Fût 11 degrees.

Wine is a matter of taste: it is as difficult to be objective about wine as it is about women, but I have tried to compensate for my own prejudices and imperfect sympathies by consulting the tastes of others, whether they have been expressed on the printed page or over the dinner-table.

If I have spent more time and space over some wines – those of Alsace, for instance – it is because I have thought the wines less familiar to many of my readers than those of Bordeaux, say, or of Burgundy. Or, as in the chapter on champagne, because it has seemed to me that an intricate process needs explaining if not only the style but the price and the presentation of the wine are to be understood.

Where I have touched at all upon the gastronomy of a region, it is only briefly – this is not a gastronomic guide – and only where there is to my mind some relevance to that region's wines.

As I am uncomfortably aware that each chapter is necessarily only the sketchiest of introductions, I have added a note on the book or books that will be found useful for the more seriously enquiring amateur. I have thought it easier for the reader to give these chapter by chapter rather than in a longer, subdivided, bibliography relegated to an appendix: a list of general and of reference books follows the first chapter.

I have recommended only recent or contemporary works, and books that should be easily available, even if out of print, at public libraries or from second-hand booksellers. (To my, author's, mind, publishers are all too ready to let books go out of print: I have written or edited twenty-seven books in my time, twenty-one of them on wine or wine and food, and all but five are out of print.) There are many other books by such authors as I have already mentioned – notably Maurice Healy and Warner Allen – that are so mannered and dated as to seem sometimes almost like parodies of themselves. Myself, I find them still readable and even in parts enjoyable, but I do not think it wise to recommend them in particular to readers of a younger generation than theirs, and mine.

In one chapter, that on champagne, I not only mention a book of my own, *Bollinger*, for recommended further reading, but draw heavily upon it for the text of the chapter itself. (I mention my *Lafite* at the end of the chapter on Bordeaux, too, but have made much less use of its material.) Much of the time I spent on that book was in Champagne in the company of experts, who painstakingly explained the complicated processes of champagne-making. I set it all down as lucidly as I could then, and see no point in rewriting it now for the sake of elegant variations in presentation. But I have shortened it, which is why I recommend the book for further study – especially as, at the time of writing, it is still in print.

To all the authors named, alive or dead, known personally to me, or only through their work, I owe a debt of gratitude. I shall not list them all here, but I must add to their names, for my especial thanks, Mademoiselle Catherine Manac'h, of the London office of Food from France, for keeping me up to date with the French laws of *appellation*, and for additions to the list of AOC and VDQS wines.

My friend and secretary, Miss Jennifer Higgie, has been, as always, a model of patience and perseverance.

Finally, to shippers and wine-merchants here in Britain, and to wine-growers, wine-brokers and shippers in France, I owe the debt that none who writes about wine is ever able to repay – for help, advice, information, encouragement and boundless hospitality.

The reader will notice inconsistencies in my use of capital initial letters for the names of wines. I am quite sure that it should be 'Champagne' the place, but 'champagne' the wine, and so, too, with 'Burgundy' and 'burgundy'. I am not so sure about 'Bordeaux' and 'bordeaux', and quite sure that 'beaujolais' looks very rum indeed.

In the first edition of this book I aimed at consistency, with such curious results as 'bâtard-montrachet' and others, very properly pointed out by Edmund Penning-Rowsell in the *Times Literary Supplement*. Now, therefore, I have thrown consistency to the winds and put down what looks right to my own eye. But there is debatable ground here between pedantry and seemliness: let the reader have pity on the poor author and, where he cannot agree, at least forgive.

CHAPTER I

France's Pride

'THE Vine's Great Nation' is the title of the chapter on France in Edward Hyams's great work, *Dionysus, A Social History of the Wine Vine*. The first chapter of the same author's slighter *Vin: The Wine Country of France* is headed, 'Nature's Vineyard'. I cannot better either phrase.

France produces not quite so much wine a year as Italy, the biggest wine-producing country in the world, but very nearly. (The two countries between them provide the world with almost half its wine.)

But she produces more fine wine than all the other countries in the world put together and, with one exception, all the table wines – red and white, sweet and dry – and the one sparkling wine by which the wines of the rest of the world are judged.

Leave out Spain's sherry and Portugal's port and madeira: these are fortified wines, and another matter. Then only the small amount of white wine produced from that part of Germany nearest to France – the Rhine and its tributaries – can be mentioned in the same breath as claret, sauternes, red burgundy, white burgundy, the wines of Alsace, of the Loire and of the Rhône, and the sparkling wine of Champagne. These are the wines that many another wine-growing country imitates, or strives to rival, without actually imitating, or to name its own wines after, and that we in the wine-drinking countries have for centuries taken as our standards of excellence.

Yet France was not the first country to make wine, nor is it to this day the country that finds it easiest.

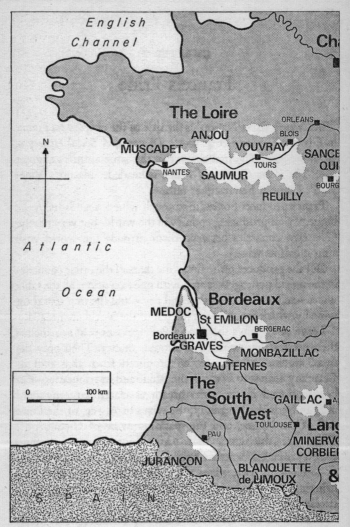

Map 1. Wine-growing areas in France

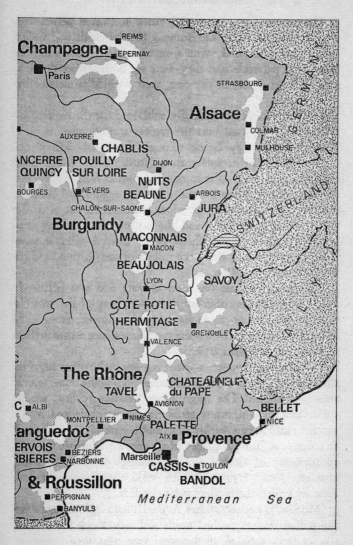

REIMS

Champagne

EPERNAY

Paris

STRASBOURG

GERMANY

Alsace

AUXERRE

CHABLIS

COLMAR

MULHOUSE

ANCERRE

POUILLY

QUINCY

SUR LOIRE

DIJON

NUITS

BOURGES

NEVERS

BEAUNE

ARBOIS

CHALON-SUR-SAONE

JURA

Burgundy

SWITZERLAND

MACONNAIS

MACON

BEAUJOLAIS

LYON

SAVOY

COTE ROTIE

HERMITAGE

ITALY

GRENOBLE

VALENCE

The Rhône

CHATEAUNEUF

TAVEL

du PAPE

C

ALBI

AVIGNON

BELLET

MONTPELLIER

NIMES

NICE

PALETTE

anguedoc

AIX

Provence

ERVOIS

BEZIERS

Marseille

RBIERES

NARBONNE

CASSIS

TOULON

& Roussillon

BANDOL

PERPIGNAN

Mediterranean   Sea

BANYULS

21

There may have been wild vines in France before the Greeks came, and then the Romans, but the Celtic and Gallic tribesmen did not make wine from their grapes; nor would it have been palatable had they done so. Some tribes drank a sort of beer; some, in any case, were forbidden alcohol by their priests.

The first vines to be specially cultivated for the making of wine were imported into the region around what is now Marseilles either by Greek colonists from Asia Minor or, earlier still by Carthaginians, from North Africa. Within two hundred years or so – the couple of centuries that straddle the dividing line between BC and AD – this region had become 'the Province', not only settled and Romanized but virtually a part of Roman Italy, and the art of wine-making was spreading north up the Rhône valley towards what is now Burgundy, and west along the valleys of the Garonne and its tributaries towards Bordeaux.

The finest, because the most delicate and best balanced, wines have always come from the periphery of the world's viticultural belts or, as Edward Hyams showed, from such heights above sea level that the vines experience a climate like that in a much higher latitude.

The grapes of sunnier, warmer regions make more sugar in the juice, which ferments into more alcohol in the wine, which means headiness. The more sugar the less acidity, which means that the wine is not refreshing, and is unbalanced. More sunshine also means thicker skins and bigger pips, which lead to coarseness. 'It is the grapes which are sweet enough to yield an adequacy of alcohol, yet acid enough to give the wine character', said Hyams, 'which yield those wines of real delicacy which the modern palate prefers.'

'Modern' is a relative term. As the Roman legions, and then the Italian traders, pushed north and west along the French river valleys, a couple of thousand years ago, they found, as did the rich Gauls whom they influenced, that the wines of the Rhône and the Garonne were more to their taste than those of Italy and Spain (whence came so many of the Roman soldiers). Strains of vine were developed that were more suitable to these regions of (by Spanish and Italian standards) cool summers and cold winters than those that the eastern and southern Mediterranean colonists had brought to Marseilles.

There were more bad years and fewer good in these more northerly latitudes than in the vineyards to the south, but the quality of the good years made it all worth while; as one of the great river systems along which the wines of Gaul were being grown had at its mouth a Mediterranean port, Marseilles, and the other an Atlantic port, Bordeaux, eventually they could be easily exported to those new markets, north and south, where the legionaries and the proconsuls were making them famous.

By the end of the Gallo-Roman era, in the fourth century AD, Ausonius, Bordeaux-born son of a Roman senator, and himself a prefect of the Empire, as well as a poet, was writing about the vineyards both of Bordeaux and of the Moselle. (Château Ausone, in the Saint Emilion, is named after him, and may or may not stand on the site of his villa.) Julian the Apostate, his contemporary, praised the wines of Paris, thus showing that the wine vine had already reached northern France. (There is still a vineyard on Montmartre.)

It is by no means improbable that at this time wine was being made for local consumption in what would now be regarded as inhospitable parts of Normandy, just as southern England grew its own wine until it became cheaper and easier to import it from France, and more profitable to grow cherries, apples and hops.

It is not necessarily the case, though, as is often stated, that in those days of poor communications, wine had to be grown in relatively unsuitable places for the sake of its sacramental purposes.

Devout Catholics such as André Simon believed, indeed, that had it not been for the Church, the successive waves of invasion from the east by Visigoths, Burgundians and Franks would have destroyed the viticulture of Gaul.

William Younger, who was more scholarly than André Simon, was also more sceptical. He was emphatic in his *Gods, Men and Wine* that, 'this theory is patently untrue. The Church had little, if anything, to do with the transmission of viticulture from the Ancient into the Christian world. Wine-growing was brought over the Dark Ages by private enterprise, and the traditions of viticulture were continued through the memories of lay wine-growers and wine-makers rather than through the manuscripts of monastic libraries.'

It seems that the vineyard area of what we must now call France actually expanded during the period that we think of as the Dark Ages ('dark' more because they are relatively un-recorded than because they were all that more benighted than the periods before and after). It was the barbarian Burgundians, from the east, who cleared the forests of what was named Burgundy after them, and planted the vine.

Some religious houses created vineyards, certainly, but others had neither the man-power nor the knowledge: their sacramental wine was provided by the gifts of the faithful, some of whom went even further in their generosity and presented vineyards, so that some that became famous as the property of this or that abbey or monastery were actually the creations of laymen.

To some small extent, then, the Church and to a greater extent the verbal tradition of the grower, kept alive in France the art and craft of wine-making. And not only kept it alive but developed and refined it. Pruning became more and more carefully considered and methodical, if not yet meet to be termed scientific, and turned the rampant climber of the south into the low, bush-like plant of the north, growing small crops that the mild summer sunshine could reach and ripen, producing small, thin-skinned, not too sweet grapes to make light wines.

Over the centuries, strains of the wine-vine were developed that were suited to the soil and the climate. And, at least as important, those parts of the thick forests of France that were being cleared for vineyards provided timber for storage.

I have written elsewhere* that although, as Edward Hyams pointed out, the wine-growers and vintners of the ancient Mediterranean and Near-Eastern worlds had known well how to make wooden casks, they long continued to use earthen amphorae, sealed with oil or with wax, for the storage of their wine. It was when wine-growing reached the more temperate regions of the north, where timber is harder and, because the climate is moister, does not dry out to brittleness in the summer, that wooden casks came into their own.

With the casks came the realization that the wine of each vintage need not be drunk within the following twelve months, but could actually be kept – and would improve with keeping, as it would, too, in the course of being shipped in wooden casks to foreign parts.

When Henry Plantagenet became Henry II of England in 1154, he was already the husband of Eleanor of Aquitaine, who brought to the marriage the greatest wine-growing region of France, with La Rochelle the port of its northern half, Bordeaux of its southern.

For the next three hundred years, until the battle of Castillon in 1453, which cost the English crown Aquitaine, the growers and shippers of the region could sell as Englishmen on the English market, reached easily by sea, whereas in France

---

*Cyril Ray, *Cognac* (Peter Davies, 1973).

itself roads were bad; there were inter-regional tolls and taxes, and bandits to boot.

And through English ports, or direct from Bordeaux and La Rochelle, they sold their wines in Scandinavia and the Low Countries, to Balts and Irishmen and Hanseatic merchants. It is from this period that the wines of France – and particularly the wines of the Bordelais – date their world fame.

*

Meanwhile, communications within France improved; markets grew at home, as well as abroad. With the expulsion of the English, the life of French kings and their courtiers became more stable, more luxurious, and Champagne – first with its still wine and then with the newly-developed sparkling – vied with Burgundy for the reigning monarch's favour as ardently as did the ladies of the court.

The tapestries and illuminated manuscripts of the period – notably the enchanting early fifteenth-century *Les Très Riches Heures du Duc de Berry* – show how skilfully and scientifically the vineyards and the vines of France were now being tilled and staked and pruned and vintaged. By the time of Henri IV (1593–1619) experts were devising improved methods of viticulture, by experiment, or importing them from northern Italy, and draining marshland, notably in the Médoc, to make vineyards in which to apply them.

By the beginning of the eighteenth century, French wines were supreme throughout the world: they were exported to Russia and the Scandinavian countries, to French settlements in Africa, India and North America. Wars with England did not interrupt the trade with Britain, which was carried on by neutral merchants and by smugglers, as it was to be later, during the wars with Revolutionary France and with Napoleon. In these latter wars, indeed, it was conducted under licences issued at high prices by the British Government to

French ships, wearing United States colours, trading through the Channel Islands.

Much of France's wealth was now invested in its vineyards, whether in those of the Bordelais, owned by old landowning families that had survived the Revolution, by the new nobility and by merchant-princes and Paris bankers, or in the small peasant holdings of Burgundy, fragments from the breaking up by the young Republic of the properties of the Church.

Napoleon was a monster who wantonly sacrificed to his ambition the lives of half his countrymen, yet his fiscal reforms left France not merely economically stable but prosperous: there was money and skill to lavish upon the nation's great wine-growing regions.

The weather was as generous, and according to André Simon, in his *The Noble Grapes and the Great Wines of France*, 'there were in all probability, more and finer wines made in France from 1830 to 1880 than had ever been made before from all the vineyards of the world. Wines were so good and there was so much of them during that blessed half century that they could be, and often had to be, kept; they were thus given a chance to show how great they could be.'

*

Then disaster struck.

Though 'struck' is not the right word, for it implies suddenness. This disaster was gradual, but no less a disaster for that. The French first found the vine-louse, *Phylloxera vastatrix*, at its deadly work in Provence in 1865, but it was slow in working its way north. It did not seriously affect the Médoc, home of the greatest clarets, until after 1878, Champagne until 1890.

George Ordish, author of the only book in English* on the blight that cost France more than the war of 1870, explained

*George Ordish, *The Great Wine Blight* (Dent, 1972).

the phylloxera in a magazine article in the centenary year of its appearance in Hammersmith:*

. . there are a number of different species of vine in the world. The European species, *Vitis vinifera*, is the only one that gives good wine. Some of the American species (they are numerous) produce grapes in abundance, for instance the Northern Fox vine, *Vitis labrusca*, but all make very poor wine, with a strong 'foxy' taste. The Phylloxera is an American insect, which lives mostly on the leaves of the American vines and does no great harm to them. It is able to inject some substance into the sap of the leaf that induces a gall to form and thus shelter the insect. The facts suggest a very ancient association between the American vines and the Phylloxera: they had evolved a form of peaceful co-existence. The insect lived mainly on the leaves, and not much on the roots, because certain vines had been selected out, by the forces of nature, with roots on which the Phylloxera could not flourish. The case was different with the European vines. *Vitis vinifera* had not evolved alongside the Phylloxera aphid, its roots had no built-in resistance. The Phylloxera attacked both leaves and roots, though it liked the roots best; it formed the usual more or less harmless galls on the leaves but had disastrous effects on the roots. The substance it injected was very active: it produced distortions which soon killed the roots and the plant died.

Eventually, the wines of France were saved by grafting her European vines on to American vine-roots, which are resistant to phylloxera – but at an enormous cost: very nearly half the country's vineyards were never replanted; small men sold out, many of them to urban *nouveaux riches*, and others cleared out of wine-growing altogether, and moved into the towns themselves.

Meanwhile, as Morton Shand explained, the shortage of wines in the lean years before the newly grafted vines were bearing, 'produced a flood of mendacious labels which either cloaked mixtures of cheap foreign wines or else chemically "improved" common French wines. Although an enormous

* *Land* (Magazine of the Shell Chemical Co.), Spring 1963.

acreage of former vineyards was definitely abandoned, the reconstruction of the remainder with grafted vines proved terribly costly, and the hard-hit owners clamoured for prohibition of the sale of wines having no title to their names.'

A series of laws on the territorial delimitation of appellations of origin passed in 1905, 1919 and 1927 culminated in the decree of July 1935 – usually referred to as *la loi Capus*, after the senator and sometime Minister of Agriculture who had been its moving spirit – which set up the Institut National des Appellations d'Origine des Vins et Eaux-de-Vie (INAO), an autonomous body upon which are represented the French Customs and Excise and the Ministries of Agriculture, Economic Affairs, Justice and Finance, along with representatives of every section of the wine trade. It has a team of its own fourteen specially trained inspectors in the government's Service de la Répression des Fraudes, to keep the trade in wine under constant surveillance, and twenty-seven similarly skilled surveyors of vineyard practice and wine-making. Its regulations are given the force of law by the Ministry of Agriculture, and it is financed by a small compulsory levy on every hectolitre of wine made in France.

The *appellation* system has done so much for the prestige of French wines, and producers in various regions outside the scheme have been so keen to be granted *appellations* for their own wines that laws of 1949, 1951 and 1955 provided for a sort of second team of *vins-à-appellation*, and the means to provide for their corporate organization, legal protection and progressive improvement. In each region, local growers set up a *Syndicat de Défense*, and these *syndicats* are organized into a Fédération Nationale des Vins Délimités de Qualité Supérieure which controls and supervizes its VDQS wines in much the same way as, and with the help of, the INAO.

A number of VDQS wines have already been moved up into the AOC class.

Proportions differ from year to year, of course, according to each year's climatic conditions for grape-growing, grape-gathering and vinification, but to take an average over the years, in every twenty bottles of wine produced annually in France at least one will be officially of VDQS standing, and at least two will be of AOC. The proportion of VDQS and AOC wines exported, of course, is much higher – very roughly about one-third to a half of French wine exports are of AOC and VDQS wines.*

The AOC and VDQS *appellations* are not in themselves, and directly, guarantees of quality, as such. What they guarantee is that the wines come from where they say they do; are made in the prescribed way, traditional and suitable to the particular region; of the proper, prescribed grapes, pruned and tended in the appropriate way; grown in suitable soil, and not in such a way as to sacrifice quality to quantity. Some years' wines will be better than those of other years – the INAO and the FNVDQS can control wine-growers and wine-makers but not the weather; not the skill or the dedication of the individual producer; or the way that casks and bottles are cared for in shippers' warehouses, wine-merchants' cellars, or on the shelves of supermarkets.

Up to that point, though, control is both detailed and rigid to an extent that would make a British farmer forget his grumbles about boards and ministries, and look upon the forms he has to fill in for the tax-gatherer as child's play.

It would take a disproportionate number of pages of this book to give in detail the way in which a bottle of AOC wine is controlled, from the soil it was grown in to its alcoholic strength when it reaches the table. A few instances must suffice:

*

*See Appendix, page 195.

For each wine, only certain types of vine are permitted. These are the so-called 'noble' grapes. Other, more prolific varieties are known as *courant*: these are not permitted in any AOC or VDQS wine, nor is any hybrid variety.*

A minimum is imposed for the alcoholic strength of each wine: it affects staying-power, and the capacity to mature.

Chaptalisation – the addition of sugar, before fermentation, to increase alcoholic strength – is forbidden in some areas, permitted in others only in bad years, on appeal from growers, and under strict control. (*Chaptalisation* does not sweeten, as the sugar ferments into alcohol: it strengthens.)

A maximum is imposed for the amount of wine to be produced per hectare.†

In most areas, and for the finest wines, vineyards may not be irrigated.

Pruning has to be done in a certain way, according to local custom.

Only certain fertilizers and insecticides are permitted.

Dates are set for the vintage.

*

*A variety may be 'noble' in one region, or for one particular *appellation*, but merely *courant* in or for another. This is because one variety may suit a particular soil or micro-climate, not another. The Gamay, for example, is *courant* in Burgundy proper, where it makes common wine, but 'noble' in the Beaujolais – southern Burgundy – where all the AOC wines are made from it.

† Before we joined the EEC, British wine-merchants would buy the good wine that came from an *appellation* area but that was surplus to the permitted amount and sell it here with the *appellation* denied to it in France. They got it cheaper than if it carried the official *acquit*, and their customers got the benefit. Nowadays, we can still buy the wine, knowing that British wine-merchants, heirs to centuries of experience, have probably chosen well; but it can no longer be labelled 'Nuits St Georges', say, if it may not be so labelled in France.

Wine with an AOC or VDQS *appellation* may not be moved – not even across a road – without an accompanying certificate, rather like a traveller abroad with his passport, and is more strictly under control than a British motorist, who has five days in which to produce a driving licence or an insurance certificate. Once a wine loses its *acquit*, it loses its claim to any particular identity.

At INAO headquarters in the Champs-Elysées, vast cadastral plans, too big in scale, at 1:2500, to be called maps, and other plans at 1:3850, show every vineyard in France with a claim to *appellation*, along with many others, alongside, to which an *appellation* would not be granted.

Morton Shand explained it:

Exposition, altitude, and latitude, together with the level of the water-table and incidental variations of soil, or in the subsoil, are what have combined to create every wine-growing area's particular micro-climate; and local variations in some of those factors may account for differences in the character of wines grown in certain districts of the same region. An outer boundary girdling the whole *appellation* must be drawn. But almost invariably there will be plots of ground inside its circumference which for one reason or another ought not to be included, even though vines may have been grown on some of them for many years. Also it rarely happens that there are not parts of a commune's planted surface which produce wine much inferior to the rest, and such parts have to be left beyond the pale. The confines of all these enclaves need to be very carefully judged. INAO has consistently refused to incorporate ground where changes in the composition of the soil are, or can become, prejudicial to quality. An important example is the denial of the *appellation* 'Bordeaux' (hierarchically the lowest for the Bordelais) to any wine grown on *Palus*, the rich alluvial deposit that covers the islands of the Gironde and forms narrow strips along the river's banks.

The illustration on page 33 is a much reduced part of one of INAO's plans.

*

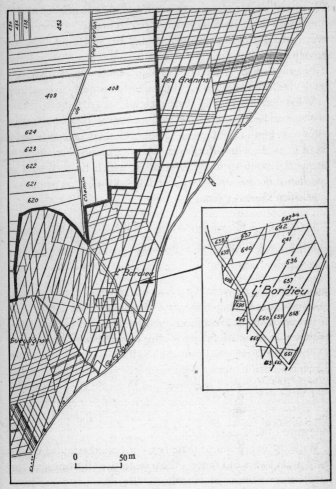

Part of a *plan de délimitation* of the INAO. Each field is planned and individually numbered. The diagonal hatching indicates areas eligible for the *appellation*, in this case that of Haut Médoc

The so-called 'Bordeaux wine scandal' of 1974 proved not so much that there are always a few rascals in every trade, however generally high-principled it may be, but how alert the French authorities are.

No fine wines – vintage or single-estate wines, that is – were affected, and no wines intended for export.

What happened was that a clever, unscrupulous wine-broker realized that there was a loophole in the law: certificates of origin did not specify colour. He switched certificates from genuine white Bordeaux (only a generic *appellation*) to cheap red wine from other regions, which he then sold as *appellation Bordeaux rouge* which commands a higher price than *appellation Bordeaux blanc*.

The loophole has been closed, and little harm has been done to consumers, but much to the Bordeaux trade – many innocents suffering for the few guilty.

*

The difference between AOC and VDQS wines is mainly one of tradition and reputation – not of stringency of control.

The AOC wines are almost entirely from the classic wine-growing regions of France – Bordeaux, Burgundy's Côte d'Or, Champagne, the Loire and the Rhône, producing wines that have been exported for centuries, and among them the noblest wines of all: Lafite, say, and Mouton; the burgundies of the Domaine de la Romanée-Conti; the finest champagnes; the lordliest white wines of the Loire and the pick of the vineyards of Châteauneuf du Pape.

With the exception of these last – the southernmost of the truly great wines of France – these wines are all from near the northernmost limits of viticulture. (Bordeaux is more temperate than its latitude would normally allow because of its Atlantic climate.) It is not so easy here as in the lusher south to grow wine at all: for wines of quality, the variety of vine matters most of all, and vineyard techniques matter a great deal. AOC regulations are particularly strict on these matters.

The VDQS wines, those that have chosen – and been chosen – to come up in the world, are from the easier south: blends of many sorts of grape have been usual, are still permitted and will go on being permitted. In this, Châteauneuf du Pape is unlike its AOC fellows, and more typical of the VDQS wines: quality is achieved by judicious blendings of wine or juice from the different local vines.

So VDQS wines are mainly from Provence, Languedoc and Roussillon; permitted yields are higher than for AOC wines and so is alcoholic strength. The judgements of tasting panels are taken into consideration, which is not the case for all AOC wines;* blending can cause flavour in a VDQS to differ widely from what locals would regard as the norm.

In many ways, VDQS wines are even more closely controlled than are AOC wines, for which long tradition and world-wide repute set standards that for the wines in the lesser league must be provided by the Federation and local pride in the product – local eyes on wider markets, too. For as prices for AOC wines climb ever higher, there are more and more opportunities for other wines, not as yet so well-known, that are prepared to set up standards, and to maintain them.

New standards, indeed, have been set for the simple wines of the south by the publication in 1974 of regulations governing the use of the *appellation* Vins de Pays.

This is a category inferior to VDQS, but strictly controlled, none the less.

A former Appellation d'Origine Simple (AOS) was abolished, and new conditions laid down for wines intended to

---

* Tasting regulations for AOC wines vary. In Bordeaux, for instance, tasting is not obligatory for Pomerol reds or for Bordeaux blanc, but is for other *appellations*. Tasting will become compulsory for AOC wines in 1980.

qualify as *vins de pays*. From 1980 they must come only from the district specified and only from authorized varieties of grape, not from hybrids; they must be vinified and cellared apart from blended or commoner wines; they must pass a tasting test, and reach a stated alcoholic strength (ranging from 9 to 10 degrees according to region).

They are unlikely to be found in Britain, but in their own regions they can be relied on as sound and reasonably consistent. The following list gives the regions they come from, but there are many permitted alternatives to each place-name: all that needs to be remembered in those parts is that the words '*vin de pays*' on a label signify that the wine has been tasted and found worthy.

Ardèche
Vin de pays du département de l'Ardèche
Vin de pays de l'Ardèche
Vin de pays des Coteaux de l'Ardèche
Aude
Vin de pays de Hauterive en pays d'Aude
Vin de pays du département de l'Aude
Vin de pays de l'Aude
Vin de pays de la Haute Vallée de l'Aude
Vin de pays du val de Dagne
Vin de pays du val de Torgan
Vin de pays du val d'Orbieu
Vin de pays de Cucugnan
Vin de pays de la vallée du Paradis
Vin de pays des coteaux de la cité de Carcassonne
Vin de pays des coteaux de Termenès

Vin de pays des coteaux de la Cabrerisse
Vin de pays des côtes de Perpignan
Vin de pays des coteaux de Peyriac
Vin de pays du Val de Cesse
Bouches-du-Rhone
Vin de pays des Sables du Golfe du Lion
Corse
Vin de pays de l'Ile de Beauté
Gard
Vin de pays des Sables du Golfe du Lion
Vin de pays des coteaux cévenols
Vin de pays du département du Gard
Vin de pays du Gard
Vin de pays des coteaux Flaviens
Vin de pays des coteaux du Salaves
Vin de pays des coteaux du Pont-du-Gard

Vin de pays du Serre de Coiran
Vin de pays des côtes du Vidourle
Vin de pays de l'Uzège
Gers
Vin de pays des côtes de Gascogne
Hérault
Vin de pays des collines de la Moure
Vin de pays des Sables du Golfe du Lion
Vin de pays du département de l'Hérault
Vin de pays de l'Hérault
Vin de pays des Côtes de Thau
Vin de pays des coteaux du Libron
Vin de pays des coteaux de Laurens
Vin de pays des coteaux de Murviel
Vin de pays des coteaux du Salagou
Vin de pays des coteaux de Peyriac
Vin de pays des côtes du Brian
Vin de pays des Gorges de l'Hérault
Vin de pays du Val de Montferrand
Loire-Atlantique
Vin de pays du départment de Loire-Atlantique
Vin de pays de Loire-Atlantique
Vin de pays de Retz
Lot
Vin de pays des côteaux de Glanes
Vin de pays du département du Lot
Vin de pays du Lot

Lot and Garonne
Vin de pays de l'Agenais
Pyrenees-Orientales
Vin de pays du département des Pyrénées-Orientales
Vin de pays des Pyrénées-Orientales
Vin de pays des coteaux de Fenouilledes
Vin de pays Catalan
Vin de pays des vals d'Agly
Tarn
Vin de pays du département du Tarn
Vin de pays du Tarn
Vin de pays des côtes du Tarn
Tarn and Garonne
Vin de pays du département du Tarn-et-Garonne
Vin de pays du Tarn-et-Garonne
Vin de pays de Saint-Sardos
Var
Vin de pays du département du Var
Vin de pays du Var
Vin de pays des côteaux Varois
Vendée
Vin de pays du département de Vendée
Vin de pays de Vendée
Vin de pays des Fiefs Vendéens
Vin de pays des Fiefs Vendéens Mareuil
Vin de pays des Fiefs Vendéens Brem
Vin de pays des Fiefs Vendéens Talmondais
Vin de pays des Fiefs Vendéens Pissotte
Vin de pays des Fiefs Vendéens Vix

THE WINES OF FRANCE

For Further Reading

ALLEN, H. WARNER, *A History of Wine*, Faber, 1961.

DION, ROGER, *Histoire de la Vigne et du Vin en France*, Paris, 1959.

HYAMS, EDWARD, *Dionysus: A Social History of the Wine Vine*, Thames & Hudson, 1965.

HYAMS, EDWARD, *Vin*, Newnes, 1959.

JEFFS, JULIAN, *The Wines of Europe*, Faber, 1971.

MORRIS, DENIS, *The French Vineyards*, Eyre & Spottiswoode, 1958.

MORRIS, DENIS, *Guide to the Pleasures of Wine*, Eyre & Spottiswoode, 1972.

ORDISH, GEORGE, *The Great Wine Blight*, Dent, 1972.

PRICE, PAMELA VANDYKE, *Eating and Drinking in France Today*, Tom Stacey, 1972.

SHAND, P. MORTON, *A Book of French Wines*, revised and edited by Cyril Ray, Penguin, 1964.

SIMON, ANDRÉ, *The Noble Grapes and the Great Wines of France* McGraw-Hill, 1957.

SIMON, ANDRÉ, *A Wine Primer*, revised edition, Penguin, 1973.

YOUNGER, WILLIAM, *Gods, Men and Wine*, International Wine and Food Society, 1966.

For Reference

BORN, WINA, *The Concise Atlas of Wine*, Ward Lock, 1974.

JOHNSON, HUGH, *World Atlas of Wine*, Mitchell Beazley, 1971.

LICHINE, ALEXIS, *Encyclopaedia of Wines and Spirits*, third, revised edition, Cassell, 1975.

CHAPTER 2

Alsace and Lorraine

ON the afternoon of 10 May 1871, in the Swan Hotel at Frankfurt-am-Main, Monsieur Jules Faure and Prince Bismarck signed a peace treaty that ceded to the four-month-old German Empire, along with an indemnity of two hundred million pounds, the *départements* of Bas Rhin and Haut Rhin, constituting the ancient province of Alsace, and the *département* of Moselle, which is that north-eastern part of the province of Lorraine that borders upon Germany and Luxembourg.

With the ceded part of Lorraine, the fortress-city of Metz; with Alsace, Strasbourg.

Of the eight statues that ring the Place de la Concorde in Paris, personifying the great provincial cities of France, that of Strasbourg was hung with black crape and crowned with *immortelles* until its liberation in 1918, to remind France of her humiliation. Not that she needed reminding.

So history has linked Alsace and Lorraine in our minds, and in the small change of conversation, for more than a century.

They are less closely linked linguistically, culturally or gastronomically – less closely, even, by geographical contiguity, for Alsace is cut off from Lorraine and the rest of France by the Vosges, and looks across the flat valley of the Rhine to Germany. (I have seen the lights of Strasbourg from a hotel near Baden-Baden.) Lorraine, on the other hand, looks down the valley of the Marne to the rest of France, cut off from Germany by the Vosges. In each case, mountains are a barrier, a river the link.

Alsace looks German: its almost excessively picturesque

villages, with their half-timbering, their overhanging gables and their storks' nests, might be Disney sets for fairy-tales far more sugary than those of the Brothers Grimm.

Alsace speaks German or, at any rate, a dialect of German. Its family names and many of its fore-names are German.

Alsace eats German. Its gastronomy is built upon the goose, its fat and its liver; on pork and on sausages; on red cabbage and white cabbage, fresh cabbage and sour – which is to say salted and fermented – cabbage. Here, in the matter of food, a major difference between Alsace and Lorraine: the Alsatian housewife cooks in lard or in goose-fat, the Lorrainer in butter.

But Alsace does not feel German: this fact, as well as its strategic importance to France, was recognized in the peace treaties of Louis XIV's time, for instance, and Napoleon's. Alsatians feel French, even if they feel a rather special sort of French, as Bretons do, and feel more French, perhaps, than do the Basques.

Two spells, not of German occupation, simply, but of incorporation first into the Kaiser's Germany, and then into Hitler's, have left unhappy memories, especially of the latter period, for this was always the most Jewish part of France, and especially as the anomalies of conscription dates in the Hitler war led to Alsatians in French uniform having brothers and cousins in German.

As to drinking, though, both Alsatians and Lorrainers share a German love of beer: the great French breweries are in Alsace and Lorraine.

The Alsatians, moreover, like the Germans of the Black Forest, and the German-speaking Swiss, make strong, dry, colourless *eaux de vie – alcools blancs*, or *schnapps* – from wild and cultivated small fruits: raspberries and strawberries, cherries and plums, elderberries and sloes, and even holly-berries.

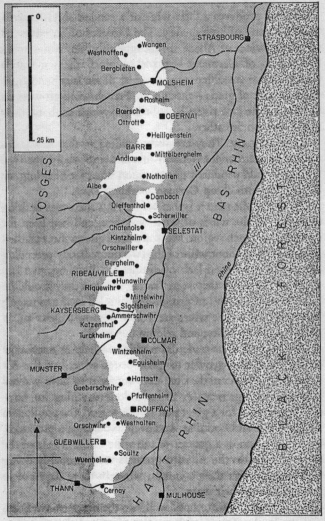

Map 2. Alsace and Lorraine

Lorraine produces a little wine of a modest sort; Alsace a great deal, and of high quality. The Moselles of Lorraine and the Rhine wines of Alsace are recognizably kin to the hocks and mosels of Germany – made to much the same style (though there are differences, as we shall see later) and from the same sort of grape – though the French wine-growers on this side of the two rivers have little for which to thank their neighbours on the other.

Or so they say. They are always telling us that it was because they were under German rule that until about 1920 the Alsatians could produce only common wine for blending, or for making into cheap German sparkling wine.

The fact of the matter is that before 1871 there was nothing to admire in the wines of what was then, and had been for centuries, a French region. Morton Shand quotes three learned English writers about wine of the two immediately preceding decades to show their lack of distinction: Redding, in 1851, wrote of them that they were 'rarely made as they should be . . . too many species of groups are mingled in the vintage'; Tovey, in 1862, 'the wines are very common'; Denman, in 1863, 'poor in quality, and seldom exported'.

The German wine trade did nothing to help or encourage the Alsatian wine-grower to grow better wine, but the Alsatian wine-grower of the time does not seem to have wanted help or encouragement, or to have done anything for himself. In any case, for a great part of this period, the phylloxera was in Alsace and Lorraine. And even so the region produced, up to 1914, almost a quarter of the wine of the whole of the German Empire: the Alsatian growers were probably doing well enough with their common wines in those days not to want to change their ways.

Nor did they need to until well into the nineteen-twenties: a clause in the Treaty of Versailles stipulated that the Germans should take for five years as much of the wines of

Alsace-Lorraine as they had absorbed when the region was part of Germany. So the growers still went on doing well enough, and the Second World War was upon us, Alsace again German, and the vineyards devastated in the course of her liberation, before the outside world had had time to realize that they had decided upon drastic change: quality not quantity.

In the nineteen-twenties, the wines of Alsace were as unfamiliar to the wine-drinkers of Britain as those of Yugoslavia were until the nineteen-forties.

George Saintsbury, whose *Notes on a Cellar-Book* appeared in 1920, wrote about Picardan and Ampurdam, Tent and La Frette, with never a word for the wines of Alsace.

They were as unfamiliar to the French. As late as the nineteen-fifties, I was staying at Château Loudenne in the Médoc and was told by old Madame Gombeau, whose late husband had been *régisseur* – farm-manager – there at the beginning of the century, how German officers had been billeted on her during the Second World War, and had brought bottles of hock back with them from leave. And the old lady told me that, 'the remarkable thing was that it came in a long narrow bottle like this, without any shoulders' – sketching a hock bottle in the air with her hands – 'I don't suppose you've ever seen such a bottle, but that's the sort they put German wines in'. And it was quite clear that not only had she never seen a bottle of German wine in her life, but never seen a bottle of Alsatian, either. Today, one sees them in every self-service grocer's shop in France.

In 1924, Warner Allen had hopes of Alsatian wines, but recorded in his *The Wines of France* only 'a number of pleasant, palatable wines, though none were great'.

Writing in 1939–40, Maurice Healy observed merely that, 'in recent years much publicity has been given to the wines of Alsace, and some of them can be quite agreeable *ordinaires*; but they have a long way to go before they can compete with the wines of the Mosel'. In the posthumous 1949 edition of Healy's *Stay Me With Flagons*, the then-famous shipper, Ian Maxwell Campbell, who edited it, was still able only to add that, 'they have undoubtedly made progress in public favour; if they continue at the same rate they will become serious rivals of Moselles'.

In his discursive books of the nineteen-fifties, Warner Allen did not mention them at all, though he mentioned almost everything else.

Yet by then other English writers on wine had referred to the Alsatian Riesling as, 'one of the most delicate and fragrant wines that exist', and to the Gewürztraminer as, at its best, 'one of the really great wines of the world'. The Alsatians had gone boldly for quality, grubbed up their common, big-yielding plants, waited patiently the five years or so before the new, 'noble' vines bore grapes for pressing; reconciled themselves to smaller yields than of old – and had triumphantly come into their own. In October 1962, *appellations d'origine* were granted to approved wines sold as 'Alsace' or 'Vin d'Alsace', to eight Alsatian wines by name of variety of grape, and to one Alsatian blend of 'noble' grapes.

Note that the *appellations* are by name of grape not, as elsewhere in France, by place-name.

This is not the only difference between Alsatian and other French wines. The resemblance to German wines is marked, as is to be expected from grapes of the same sort, grown in much the same way, in much the same climate. Alsatian white wines (the pinks and reds are negligible, both in quality and style) are much more like hocks and Mosels than they are like white burgundies, say, or white Bordeaux. They are a little more like Loire wines than these, but still much nearer to the German.

Yet they are still different from these, if less so. Alsatians ferment out their wines much more fully than the Germans do, so that they retain fragrance but become drier: they are spicy, yet crisp, aromatic wines that go admirably with the rich food of the region, and yet they never cloy, as a full Palatinate hock can, or a great wine from the Rheingau. They are charmers, and as the charm is in their freshness they should be drunk young. (There are a very few, full, rich Alsatian wines, similar to the German *auslesen* or *beerenauslesen*, usually labelled 'Réserve' or 'Réserve Exceptionelle', and these benefit from bottle-age. But they rarely come one's way.)

Another resemblance to German wines lies in the bottle, the *flûte d'Alsace*. (One French writer claims that the Germans 'stole' their own tall, tapering bottle from Alsace: this is nonsense.) It is always green, like the German bottle for Mosels, never brown like that of the hocks, and is very slightly – imperceptibly – bigger.

Although *appellation* goes by grape-name, not by place, it is generally agreed that of the almost sixty-mile long and mile or so wide *vignoble*, or wine-growing region (stretching from Thann, west and a little north of Mulhouse, to Marlenheim, west and a little south of Strasbourg, with Colmar and Séléstat dividing the strip into three), the region south of Barr produces on the whole the finer wines, with Riquewihr and Ribeauvillé the best-known producing communes, and Colmar the centre of the trade.

It used to be said of the wine of the Rangen vineyard, near Thann, in southern Alsace, that it 'makes a person quickly drunk, and as quickly attacks the nerves', but that was in the days when Alsace was Elsass, and a part of the Kaiser's Empire.

Another emperor, the first Napoleon, is quoted by one writer as having said of the wine of Wolxheim, at the other end of the region, that it was '*mon vin préferé*', and by another as having said that it would break a man's legs under him. I do not know whether these judgements are contradictory or not.

Some 30,000 acres of vines in Alsace are divided among 10,000 peasant proprietors, which is why few single vineyards are at all well-known. The growers seldom do their own pressing and vinification, but send their grapes to cooperatives, to the few bigger estates, or to the presses of big producer-shippers.

The names of such firms are important guides, therefore, to style, reliability and quality: a few individual houses are mentioned later in this chapter, and any good wine-merchant is able to recommend others. In any case, the general level is high: I cannot recall having drunk a badly-made Alsatian wine – even the most modest, though at worst they can be very slight, always have at least a touch of the characteristic Alsatian style, and a clean finish.

THE WINES OF ALSACE

The following are the *appellations contrôlées* granted to Alsatian wines:

Alsace or Vin d'Alsace

The white wine of the region, in its most modest aspect, usually that made from the Chasselas or Sylvaner grape, or a blend, but grown in delimited – because traditional – wine-growing areas of the region; gathered after a certain prescribed date; and made in the traditional way. Often sold under a brand name, such as 'Flambeau d'Alsace', or 'Chevalier d'Alsace', along with the *appellation*.

Even though a wine is entitled only to a 'Vin d'Alsace' *appellation* it must still conform to rigorous standards: a wine made from an unacceptable grape (a hybrid, for instance) or even an acceptable grape grown in an unsuitable soil, or made before the prescribed time or in a non-traditional way, may not be sold as anything but a *vin blanc* simply, or under a trade name without *appellation*. A vin d'Alsace made from a blend of permitted grapes may be styled 'Edelzwicker'.

Chasselas

An approved, but not a very highly regarded grape. A wine *could* be labelled 'Chasselas: Appellation Vin d'Alsace Contrôlée', but I have never seen one such. Alsatian wine made from this grape would be called 'Vin d'Alsace', simply; given a brand name; or (especially if blended, probably with the noble Sylvaner) sold as 'Vin d'Alsace Edelzwicker'.

Even this most modest of the *appellation* wines of the region has some of the characteristic Alsatian freshness and charm, though it lacks the elegance of the Riesling and the fragrance of the Gewürztraminer, and is not so crisply refreshing, because of lack of acidity, as most of its better-born neighbours.

Edelzwicker

A blend that must be only of grapes entitled to the *appellation contrôlée*.

Gewürztraminer

Gewürz means 'spicy': the Gewürztraminer is an even fuller-flavoured, more fragrant selection bred from the full and fragrant traminer, a name no longer used.

Denis Morris says, in his *Guide to Wine*, that Gewürztraminer is, 'particularly popular with Parisian women'. I have not, alas, been able to conduct my researches with quite such scholarly assiduity.

Certainly, the Gewürztraminer has an immensely strong – sometimes almost vulgarly opulent – bouquet. It is said that one can smell a good example when the glass is four inches from the nose, but this is to underestimate the fragrance: I have known an opened bottle and a glassful to scent a whole small dining-room – one knew what was in the glass as one opened the door.

Yet although the wine smells intensely sweet, and is as strong in flavour – what one might well call a *heavy* wine – it should usually be dry in the mouth. So it stands up well to the richest stews and sauces. Alexis Lichine goes so far as to suggest drinking it with curry – French 'curries', or dishes *à l'Indienne*, are much milder than the curries usually served in this country, though a friend tells me that there are Indian (or Pakistani) restaurants in London that specialize in the lightly spiced dishes of the North-West Frontier, and that Gewürztraminer goes well with them.

Alsatians like to drink Gewürztraminer with their truffled Strasbourg *pâté de foie gras*, on the principle of rich wine with rich food, in the same way as the Bordelais drink Sauternes with their *pâté de foie gras des Landes*. Myself, I prefer a sharper wine with so rich a dish.

Note, though, that I said that this wine is *usually* dry. The Gewürztraminer ripens earlier than the Riesling, which is quite the most widely grown vine of the region, and the Sylvaner, the next most widespread. In a poorish year, Rieslings and Sylvaners may have to be picked before they are fully ripe, and will give thinnish, sharpish wine: the Gewürztraminers may well be ripe and give better results. In a good year, though, when the Rieslings and Sylvaners come into their own, the Gewürztraminers may be left to become overripe and attacked by the *pourriture noble*, the 'noble rot' that makes the great lusciously sweet wines of Sauternes,* and the German *Trockenbeerenauslesen*.

Such wines are rare in Alsace, but they do exist: they are splendid dessert wines, and inevitably expensive.

*See page 151.

Goldriesling
Knipperlé
These, like the Chasselas (q.v.) are among the less distinguished
varieties of grape. No wines that I know of are sold under
these names: the wines are used to blend for Zwicker (q.v.).

Muscat
Like the Gewürztraminer, Muscat is luscious on the nose, dry
in the mouth. Some connoisseurs, Fritz Hallgarten among
them, rate a really fine Muscat as the equal of the best Gewürztraminer, but André Simon found that the bouquet promised
a better-bred, less earthy, wine than it showed itself to be on
the palate.

Pinot Blanc
I have very seldom come across this wine, though it is entitled to an *appellation*, and it has its admirers. André Simon
preferred it to the Muscat, as having less bouquet, but more
body and distinction. When I have drunk it I have thought it
nearest in style to the Sylvaner. Also known as the Klevner.

Pinot Gris
Dry, with less crispness than the Riesling, more body and
fruit; it sometimes shows a pinkish tinge. Sometimes known
as Tokay d'Alsace, though there is no connection with the
great wine of Hungary. Like Muscat, used for blending with
commoner wines to produce Edelzwicker, or wines sold
under brand-names.

Pinot Noir, or Pinot Noir Rosé d'Alsace
A certain amount of red and a good deal more pink wine is
made in Alsace for local consumption: these are nothing to
write home about, and no Alsatian of my acquaintance has a
good word to say for them, but if made from this grape they

are entitled to an *appellation*. In this German-speaking region, the rosé is often labelled *Schillerwein*.

Riesling

This, whatever the amateurs of Gewürztraminer may say, is to my mind the monarch of all Alsatian wines. At its best, it has a balance of fruitness and acidity that is both refreshing and yet satisfying, with a delicacy of fragrance and flavour that makes the Gewürztraminers brashly obvious in their appeal. At its worst, in a poor year, it could be thin and insipid, but *chaptalisation** is permitted in Alsace.

Of course, there are Rieslings and Rieslings. Much, as in all Alsatian wines, depends on the shipper (which is to say, in these parts, the maker, of the wine: he grows some of his own grapes and buys others from smaller growers). Hugel, perhaps the biggest of the Alsatian wine-houses, have not sacrificed quality to size: their reputation is justifiably high. Preiss, Zimmer and Trimbach are smaller firms that are highly thought of. Dopff au Moulin, who make, incidentally, a particularly good Alsatian sparkling wine,† are not to be confused with Dopff and Irion, though both are sound firms. Schlumberger's wines come from farther south than those of some of the other great houses, between Colmar and Mulhouse, and it is perhaps because of this that they tend to be softer, with more southern sunshine in them, than others. I remember a late-gathered (Réserve Spéciale) Pinot Gris of theirs being served some years ago with a confection of peaches and cream at a Wine and Food Society dinner: it was sweet enough on the nose and the palate, yet acid enough not to be as cloying as a great sweet German wine or Sauternes might have been.

This brings me to the other two factors that determine the

*See page 31.
†See page 51.

style or the quality – or both – of an Alsatian wine: provenance and picking. On the whole, labels do not specify vineyard sites, but some are important enough to be named: they are infrequently met with, and it would be confusing to list them here, but it is worth bearing in mind that most of the best wines come from Colmar northwards to Bergheim, or southwards to Guebwiller.

Sylvaner

More common than the Riesling, and softer, with less acidity, this wine is the cheapest of the *appellation contrôlée* wines of Alsace to bear the name of a noble grape – bland yet refreshing, easy to drink, and almost always very good value.

*

Sparkling Wine

A little sparkling wine is made in Alsace. It is not granted any *appellation* other than those that apply to still wines – the name of the region and the grape. So far as I know only one house, that of Dopff au Moulin, makes a sparkling wine by the champagne process,* and this, of course, is entitled to the words '*méthode champenoise*' on its label.

THE WINES OF LORRAINE

There was a time, before the Champagne riots of 1911,† when wine was sent from Lorraine to Reims and Epernay to be made into champagne. Then wine-growing virtually died out. Recently, though, there has been something of a revival, and if there are no fine wines yet – in this part of France, beer is best – the most beautiful wine-glasses in the world are made here, at the tiny town of Baccarat (where the enchanting mid-

*See Chapter 3, page 71.
†Cyril Ray, *Bollinger* (Peter Davies, 1971).

nineteenth-century paperweights were made that fetch such fantastic prices at Christie's and Sotheby's) itself not far from the pottery-making town of Lunéville.

The wines of Lorraine do not aspire to be worthy of the glasses of Baccarat – none has been granted an *appellation*, but VDQS status was accorded in 1951 to two local wines, unknown outside the region, but pleasant with summer picnics and at village restaurants.

Edward Hyams,* indeed, wrote of them as 'excellent, delicate, dry, pale wines, some almost green, superlatively refreshing on hot days, good to drink with meals or courses of fish . . .' Perhaps 'excellent' and 'superlatively' are going it a bit, but it is clear that Edward Hyams enjoyed himself in Lorraine.

Côtes de Toul
So-called *vin gris*, but actually pale pink or even a soft golden, very dry wine from the eastern slopes of the Meuse, to the west and south-west of Toul.

Vins de la Moselle
These include wines similar, but inferior, to the Sylvaners, Gewürztraminers and Rieslings of Alsace; pale pink wines from near Metz, often called Clairet de Moselle; and *vins gris* like those of Toul. Various grapes are permitted, among them Gamay, the various Pinots, Meuniers and Auxerrois.

All, to my taste, tend to be thin and sharp: none that I know of is exported.

For Further Reading

HALLGARTEN, S. F., *Alsace and its Wine Gardens*, Second edition, Wine & Spirit Publications, 1969.

*Edward Hyams, *Vin* (Newnes, 1959).

CHAPTER 3

Champagne

WHAT is probably the most famous, certainly the most festive, wine in the world comes from some 40,000 acres of vineyards in the *département* of Marne, consisting of three contiguous parts.

One lies on the southern-facing slopes of the Montagne de Reims – a mountain so-called: it is a system of chalk downs rising to no more than six hundred feet above the surrounding countryside; one is a nine-mile stretch of the Vallée de la Marne, also facing south, across the river; the third is the Côte des Blancs, running south from Epernay, on the Marne, for about a dozen miles, and facing east.

As its name indicates, this third region grows white grapes, the other two grow black, and this is roughly the usual proportion of black to white in each bottle of champagne, which is a blended wine. A *blanc de blancs* champagne, made only from white grapes, is a relative rarity, as will be seen later.

The Pinot Noir and the White Chardonnay are the two chief grapes permitted by law to a wine if it is to be called 'champagne'. The Meunier is also permitted and fairly widely used, though not by the best houses; two other minor strains are not forbidden, but are not being replanted, and by now account for less than 1 per cent of the region's wines.

(There are small and unimportant outlying patches, west along the Marne towards Paris, which is a hundred miles away, and south-east along the upper reaches of the Marne and Aube, towards Troyes. It is here that the inferior strains are still grown.)

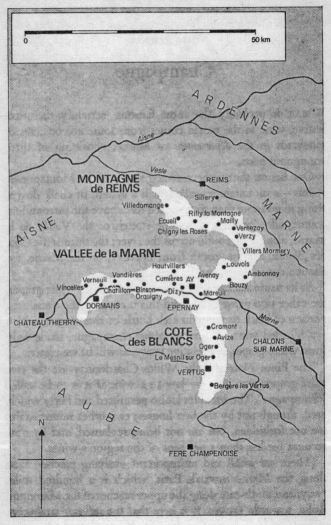

Map 3. Champagne

Epernay, at the very heart of the region, and Reims, a couple of miles beyond it to the north, are the two centres of the champagne trade.

It is all smoothly undulating downland country, similar to, and indeed part of, the same chalk system as that of Kent and Sussex, and less than a couple of hundred miles south-east of its nearest point at Dover. It is the northernmost wine-growing region of France and, except for the Mosel and the less important reaches of the Rhine, the northernmost wine-growing region in the world.

The juice of grapes grown in a cool climate tends to ferment slowly; fermentation is often not complete when the cold winter weather comes, checking the transformation of grape-sugar into alcohol. Then, with the spring, and the warmer weather, there is a tendency to a secondary fermentation. This phenomenon is frequently met with in young German wines, which show a subdued effervescence – a quality which the Germans describe as being *spritzig*, the French as being *pétillant*. Champagne is made by encouraging and controlling this tendency, and inducing a full secondary fermentation in bottle during the spring following the vintage.

This vintage takes place at the end of September or early October: the date is decided by the Comité Interprofessionel du Vin de Champagne.

Some of the big champagne firms with world-famous names own no vineyards at all; none has enough to satisfy its requirements; every house buys some or all of its grapes from small growers.

Every year, the Comité Interprofessionel, which represents growers, shippers and other sections of the trade, fixes prices for the grapes, based on a fixed scale which has long been established. The Ay, Cramant and Verzenay vineyards, for example, are fixed at 100 per cent: all that the committee needs to do is to settle what 100 per cent is for the year and every grower, down to the man far away in the Aube, at 75 per cent, knows the official price.

This is one of the main factors in deciding style and quality – whether a big firm's average price for the grapes in its blend is about 95 per cent or about 80.

Another deciding factor is that the law permits the *appellation* 'champagne' to the juice of three pressings of the grapes. The best champagne is made only from the juice of the first and, to give body, part of the second. Big firms with a high reputation for quality sell the remainder of the second pressing, and all the third, to lesser firms making cheaper champagne, who will blend it with first pressings of cheaper grapes. (A fourth pressing is allowed only to be made into *vin ordinaire*, usually given to the workmen as part of their ration; the residual solid matter of pressed skins, pips and stalks is sold to distillers to be made into *eau de vie de marc*, generally known as *marc*, simply.)

First fermentation takes place in cask, and not in a cellar, but a *cellier* (an underground cellar is in French *une cave*; *un cellier* is an above-ground shed or store-room such as in Spain is a *bodega*, in Bordeaux *un chai*). The casks are not sealed until first fermentation is complete; then, after some three weeks of rest for what is now a dry, still wine, it is suddenly chilled, either by letting in the cold, outside air – for it is now the year's end – or more usually nowadays by air-conditioning devices.

In the spring, cultivated grape yeasts are added to the wine along with sugar – not for sweetening but for the yeasts to feed upon and turn into alcohol and the carbonic gas that gives the wine its bubble as soon as it is in bottle – which it is within a matter of hours.

The wine is now in the bottles or magnums – double bottles – in which it will eventually reach the consumer. (Champagne is not usually *made* in double magnums, except

I think by Bollinger, nor in bigger bottles; nor is it *made* in quarter-bottles. It is decanted from bottles of standard size and from magnums into especially big or especially small bottles.) The bottles are not yet carrying the corks, though, that their purchasers will pop. Before the champagne is ready for drinking, it must be rid of its sediment, and this will require that one cork be removed and another take its place.

Nowadays, the first cork, the *bouchon de tirage*, is usually a metal crown cap, lined with cork or plastic: this will be replaced by the strong, bulbous-headed, wired-on *bouchon d'expédition* after the two processes of *remuage* and *dégorgement*.

One or two small old-fashioned firms who are dedicated to quality still use a *bouchon de tirage* the same size and shape as the final cork. One can tell from the bottle which has been used. The bottle that was crown-corked until freed from sediment, and then recorked, will have a *bague couronne* – a crown ring – like this:

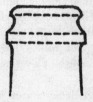

whereas the bottle that had the old-fashioned *bouchon de tirage* the same size and shape as the second and final cork will have a *bague carré* or square-sectioned ring, like this:

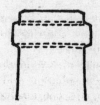

First, the bottles are left on their sides, for anything between the one year required by law and as much as five years, according to the firm. During this period, the secondary fermentation is taking place, causing bubbles in the wine, and a fine sediment is settling along the lower side of the bottle, formed of exhausted yeast cells and solids from the wine.

The bubbles must be retained, the sediment removed.

Two processes are required to get rid of the sediment: *remuage*, or riddling, and *dégorgement* – disgorgement.

The bottles are placed, neck downwards up to the shoulder, in racks, called *pupitres* (pulpits), standing in inverted Vs, so slotted that each bottle can be placed pointing downwards at an angle, and the slots so bevelled that the angle of the bottles can be changed from almost completely horizontal to almost completely vertical. First, they are left for three weeks, to let the sediment drop, and then they are thus changed, over the weeks, for some three to five months, by *remueurs*, the most highly-skilled and the highest-paid workers in the cellars, who rotate, oscillate and tilt each bottle by incredibly quick movements of their huge, yet precisely accurate hands – hands so accurately controlled, indeed, as to be able to move each bottle an eighth of a turn, no more, no less, with each movement.

A skilled *remueur* can rotate 40,000 bottles, and oscillate 20,000 of them, in a working day, his hands flickering at a fantastic rate over the *pupitre*. As each bottle is rotated, at an eighth of a turn at a time, through a number of circles, being shaken at the same time, and its angle of tilt increased, so that eventually it is almost vertical, cork downwards, with the sediment now adhering to the bottom of the cork, and the wine perfectly clear.

This makes disgorgement possible, briskly effected by artificially freezing the neck of the bottle, thus solidifying the sediment, which flies out as a virtually solid piece of sand-coloured stone when the machine, if a crown cork has been used, or, in the old-fashioned way, the *dégorgeur* releases the cork. The *dégorgeur* holds the bottle against the light; sniffs; and leaves the bottle underneath a spring-loaded temporary cork to keep in the gas until the next operation.

But between popping the cork and putting his thumb over the bottle after the sediment has been discharged, he has deliberately allowed a little of the froth to escape – partly to carry with it any loose specks of sediment still clinging to the inside of the neck of the bottle, partly to increase very slightly the space left by the discharge of the sediment and of the minute amount of frozen wine immediately below it.

(I describe the operation as it is done by hand: although the machine simplifies and expedites the process, it remains basically the same.)

This space has to be refilled, and the character and style of a particular brand of champagne depend very largely on how this is done. Partly, the bottle is topped up with some of the same wine as that already in the bottle: partly, there is the allied process of *dosage*, or liqueuring – the adding of a further amount of the same wine in which has been dissolved some cane sugar. This mixture is the *liqueur d'expédition*, and it determines how sweet or how dry the particular champagne will be.

All champagne is dry by nature, and much the more so because it has been fermented not once, but twice, so that all residual sugar is consumed by yeasts.

In the very best champagnes, what the *dosage* does is ever so slightly to soften the austerity of perfect dryness, leaving the wine still crisply dry, but not astringently so. It can also be the means of deliberately making the champagne into a sweet wine, for there are those, such as Russian grand dukes in the old days and, today, South American tycoons and some Oriental potentates, who always prefer their champagne to be sweet; others who enjoy (as I do) a glass of sweet champagne with a peach or a pear after one of those infrequent champagne dinners – which, to my mind, should be preceded by a dry non-vintage wine, accompanied by a fuller, but still dry, vintage, and end with sweet. Not that I am so fond as my *Champenois* friends are of champagne as a wine for all courses, nor do many of them ever serve sweet champagne at all: it is the custom of the country to serve old, dry champagne with fruit and puddings, which is not to my taste nor, I think, to that of most Englishmen.

Another service that liqueuring can perform, if it is pretty generous, though not yet enough to make the wine truly sweet, is to mask the inadequacies of a thin wine, made perhaps from the cheapest grapes or from as many pressings as are legally permitted, or from both. *Dosage* can cover a multitude of sins.

And over all, of course, it is one of the factors, along with the choice of grapes, the blending of black grapes and white grapes and of this vineyard and that and, in non-vintage wines, of the wines of different years, that determine the house 'style' of a champagne. Among the very best dozen or so champagnes, some are drier than others, some sweeter; some are lighter, some are fuller-flavoured. And those that are sweeter are not necessarily *sweet* – it makes more sense to say that they are marginally less dry than others. The very good Lanson Black Label, for instance, is just such a non-vintage wine: the exact amount of its liqueuring varies, of course, each year, according to the quality of the grapes, but it usually has about $\frac{1}{4}$ per cent more than the driest champagnes. I often choose it when entertaining those who say that champagne is 'too acid', while finding it, myself, by no means unacceptably sweet.

The amount of liqueuring is expressed in terms of a percentage, but this is not, as is sometimes supposed, the amount of sugar as a percentage of the total amount of champagne.

The percentage is worked out to a complicated technical formula but, very roughly, the figure is that of how many centilitres of the liqueur – half sugar, half old champagne – in the 78 centilitres that go to a bottle. The actual amount of *sugar* would be *half* the percentage figure.

Bollinger is a particularly dry wine, because liqueuring is kept to the absolute minimum. As Patrick Forbes observes, in his classic book, *Champagne*, 'In general it may be said that sweetening conceals the quality and masks the defects of a champagne; the really great ones are therefore seldom sweetened to any appreciable extent . . .'

I have been told by the shipper of a very famous *marque* that no champagne is entirely without sugar: that such a wine would be unacceptably dry. He did not know his competitors' secrets, for Bollinger did entirely without liqueuring on three occasions between 1945 and 1965 – in 1947, in the premium quality 1959, and in one non-vintage blend. Its post-war average has been between $\frac{1}{2}$ and $\frac{3}{4}$ per cent, and in the 'big' year of 1964 it was only $\frac{1}{4}$ per cent.

The most nearly comparable champagne to Bollinger in style is Krug, who added $\frac{1}{2}$ per cent in 1959 and $\frac{3}{4}$ per cent in 1961. Leaving specific years aside, and looking at averages to compare with Bollinger's over the years of between $\frac{1}{2}$ and $\frac{3}{4}$ per cent, Pol Roger's average over recent years has been given as $1\frac{1}{4}$ per cent, Moët et Chandon's $1\frac{1}{2}$, Lanson's $1\frac{3}{4}$ per cent. These are figures for the various houses' vintage wines: Lanson Black Label, the firm's non-vintage, is about 2, and I have no doubt that the *dosage* of the non-vintage wines of the other houses would also be higher than that of their vintage.

Many houses are more reluctant to give figures of *dosage*, but I should say that over the *grandes marques* as a whole the average for the driest wines (labelled, as a rule, 'Brut' or 'Extra Dry') is about $1\frac{1}{2}$ per cent.

Fully sweet champagnes (usually labelled 'Rich') run to

about 4 per cent liqueuring. Not every house makes such a wine and some of those that are made are not exported to Britain. Bollinger, for instance, make a *Carte Blanche*, with a 4-per-cent *dosage*, but only for the South American market. This is much the same as those sweet champagnes that are sold on the British market – Lanson Rich and Veuve Clicquot Rich – and a little more than the Pol Roger Rich, which is more like $3\frac{1}{2}$ per cent. All very modest compared with what I am told pre-revolutionary noblemen in St Petersburg used to demand – a champagne with a *dosage* of 12 per cent. One would have thought it would have stuck to the sides of the slippers of the Maryinsky ballerinas.

*

Of the total output of champagne over a period of years, some 15 per cent is vintage, the rest non-vintage.

There is a sense in which non-vintage champagne, of any of the great houses, is really the true, classic wine in that, being essentially a blend, it reflects the ideas, ideals and character of the people who make it. For their choice of how much black and how much white, from which vineyards of what region, how much of one year's reserves and how much of another, is a more deliberate expression of the personality of their house than is possible in their vintage champagne, where some of the character is imposed by influences over which they have no control.

Vintage champagne is also, of course, a blended wine in that it is made of black and white grapes from different vine-yards: but it is made of the grapes of one year's vintage only. It must be a 'good' year – which can, but does not necessarily, mean a plentiful year, but must mean a year that produced grapes of fine quality: all fully ripe at vintage time, with plenty of sugar and flavour in the fruit. This means a richer, but not, of course, a sweeter wine, for the sugar is converted by fermentation into alcohol – heavier in style, fuller in flavour. It will not only reflect the style of the house that made it, but also the character of the year: a very full, rich 1959, for instance, or a much lighter and more delicate 1952 or 1962.

So whereas any particular firm's non-vintage is unique – solely and specifically a creation of that one firm, its 1966, say, will share the characteristics of 1966, to however slight a degree, with the 1966 of other houses. A good firm is immensely proud of its vintage wine, but may well be in a sense prouder of its non-vintage: it requires even greater skill and subtlety in the blending and making (as a rule, that is: there are occasional 'difficult' vintage years), and it reflects even more precisely the character and personality of its makers.

Why, then, do the great firms trouble to make a vintage champagne at all, and why is it dearer than non-vintage?

Although it is hard to get any champagne-maker to say as much or, at any rate, to say it for quotation, I believe that many of the finest houses would be glad to devote all their skill and all their resources to producing the best non-vintage wines they are capable of producing; to have the fine wine of vintage years in reserve to blend with, and to better, the non-vintage; and to be judged by them.

Each *grande marque* house produces a vintage wine in a vintage year because its rivals do, and because it is a means of getting talked and written about. It is dearer than non-vintage because it takes up so much of the highest-quality wines that would otherwise make it easier to blend the non-vintage.

Besides declaring with a flourish the appearance of each vintage wine, some firms have each taken a further step towards attracting publicity and – they hope – acquiring prestige: the production and promotion of premium or *de luxe* brands. These are champagnes that are said to be superior to the vintage wines of each house, as the vintage is superior to the non-vintage, and appropriately more expensive still.

Some, like the Dom Pérignon of Moët & Chandon, are blended differently from other wines of the same house: Dom Pérignon is said to reverse the usual proportions of black grapes and white, and be (it may vary a little, according to the year) about 75 per cent white, 25 black – almost a *blanc de blancs*.

Others, like the Taittinger 'Comtes de Champagne', are, in fact, *blanc de blancs*; others are said to be *tête de cuvée* – made only from the first pressing of the grapes, whereas even the usual *grande marque* champagne takes along with the juice of the first pressing some of the second pressing to add character and body to the first.

Bollinger stick to their usual style and quality, but take from the reserves of undisgorged vintage wine, fine wines of great vintages, about ten or twelve years old, and disgorge them for commercial distribution under a special label giving the dates both of vintage and of disgorgement, and designated 'R.D.' – *récemment dégorgé*, or 'recently disgorged'.

Normally, Bollinger vintage wines are taken off their sediments some four or five years after bottling, and even this is long by champagne standards.

A longer spell even than that on its sediment means greater softness and mellowness in champagne – and, of course, a higher price, because of the capital that has been tied up in the cellar.

There is usually a bigger jump in price from vintage to premium quality, or '*super-de-luxe*', than from non-vintage. It is worth remembering that the duty, both in France and abroad, is exactly the same on all sparkling wine, whether non-vintage, vintage or de luxe: thus, the actual price differential is proportionately greater than it appears.

Some of these *de luxe* wines are most beautifully packaged

and presented: Dom Pérignon, in a replica of an eighteenth-century champagne bottle with its pastiche of an eighteenth-century label, must be the most handsome bottle of wine in the world, and the Roederer Cristal Brut, in the clear-glass bottle that Tsars used to insist upon, is historically interesting as well as visually appealing. There are others that are vulgar beyond belief.

Most champagne-lovers would agree that the *de luxe* brands are for Christmas presents to (or from) rich uncles; that vintage champagne is for special occasions or, as it is usually fuller in flavour than non-vintage, for those who like, and can afford, to drink champagne throughout a meal; and that non-vintage of a good brand is the classic champagne, and the finest of all before-meal or between-meal drinks.

To say 'of a good brand' is of course to beg the question. There are a couple of dozen well-known firms, at least, the products of which differ only in style, not in quality, so that choosing between them is a matter of personal taste: some are drier, some a little less dry, some are light and 'crisp', some fuller-bodied.

There is no such precise definition of the *grandes marques* champagnes as there is of the *crus classés* – the named greatest single-vineyard wines – of Bordeaux. There is a Syndicat de Grandes Marques that adds to its number by election; there are some firms that seem to decide for themselves that they are *grandes marques*, and no one to say them nay.

But there are twelve firms the qualifications of which are unassailable *in Britain*: the twelve champagne houses that in 1956, regarding themselves then as the leading firms shipping to Britain under their own labels – leading not necessarily in quantity, though their shipments had to be sizeable – established the Champagne Academy. These twelve, without at all disparaging other notable firms, regard themselves as the *grandes marques*.

Every year, their British agents each select a young member of the wine or the catering trade (always from a firm other than their own) to undergo a fortnight's course in Champagne, each staying at one of the principal's houses, seeing the vintage and the cellar-work, and visiting bottle and cork factories. There is an examination that takes some passing, and a diploma that is worth having.

A very few – very few indeed – of the most eminent firms are outside the scheme, and there are some outside that are bigger than some that are inside, but in any debate about which are the *grandes marques*, it is well to know that the twelve that founded the Champagne Academy are, in alphabetical order:

Bollinger	Mumm
Charles Heidsieck	Perrier-Jouët
Heidsieck Dry Monopole	Pol Roger
Krug	Pommery
Lanson	Roederer
Moët et Chandon	Veuve Clicquot

It is well to remember, though, that there may be some very good firms that could never reach any such list as being too small, and that others may well make very good wine indeed but sell most of it in France.

Note, too, that these are firms that ship under their own labels. Other firms specialize in BOB – 'Buyer's Own Brand' – champagnes that are bought by retail wine-merchants, the wine departments of department stores, London clubs and so on, to carry their own label and their own name and be sold rather more cheaply than the well-known marques. Some are good, sound wines; none is in the same class as the wines that the leading houses sell under their own names. This is where the secondary pressings and the cheaper grapes go, which is not to say that they cannot be well-made, skilfully blended and honestly marketed. It is not unusual for the same BOB wine to be sold under half a dozen different names by half a dozen different retail firms.

Finally, there is the wine made by *manipulants*.

There are said to be 144 champagne firms making the traditional blended wine, each with their own brand-name or names; and 15,000 vineyard owners, of which number 3000 are *manipulants*, making their own wine from their own vineyards. Some of these wines can be bought by the roadside, as motorists in England buy eggs or strawberries. Some that are made on a big enough scale may also become BOB brands; some find their way into the village shop or the local restaurant.

They vary enormously in quality. As André Simon pointed out in *The History of Champagne*:

The wines sold by shippers and *vignerons* are by no means the same, although they are all made within the legal limits of the *delimitation* and are all equally entitled to the name of Champagne. They differ basically on account of the difficulty for the *vignerons* of making Champagne in the traditional manner: . . . that is, the happy blending of wines made from grapes in different Champagne vineyards. In many cases, this is impossible for them. Most *vignerons* have no choice but to sell the Champagne made from the grapes of their own vineyards . . .

Champagne from the grapes of one Champagne village can indeed be very good, but Champagne made from a blend of black and white Pinots,* some from the Montagne de Reims vineyards, some from the Valley of the Marne, and some from the Côte des Blancs, is a much better wine, more balanced, more complete and more lasting, not merely keeping alive for a greater number of years, but gaining power as well as charm with age. The 'single' Champagne of most *vignerons* is not made to last: it is made to be drunk as soon as possible, when

---

* *Sic:* It is now recognized that the white champagne grape, the Chardonnay, sometimes called, as here by André Simon, the Pinot Chardonnay, is not a Pinot at all.

its freshness and lower cost are very real assets ... a cheaper Champagne than that which bears the famous name of one of the *Grandes Marques*.

*

So there are differences in quality among champagnes in general, as there are differences in style between the most distinguished.

It can be argued that there is no bad champagne – that the strict control by INAO, exercised both directly and through the Comité Interprofessionel du Vin de Champagne, ensures that all champagne is good, though some is better than others. Or that control is exercised only over material (the grape), method and provenance, leaving room for some pretty thin stuff.

All would agree, though, that champagne at its best, or at its most characteristic, is a gay wine and the cause of gaiety in those who drink it. Not only do the very bubbles laugh at one: they carry the alcohol into the bloodstream more quickly than happens with a still wine – one gets an immediate 'lift' or 'kick' from champagne but, so long as it is not a heavily sugared wine, there is little to pay for it next day in the form of a hangover. Champagne is light in texture, body and taste (though its alcohol content is usually a little higher than that of a claret) so that it is easy both on the head and the stomach.

It is the clean finish, fresh in the mouth, that makes champagne such a good *apéritif*: it is the immediate tonic effect of the quickly released alcohol that makes it such a good pick-me-up and so good at a party. John Jorrocks said, nearly a century and a half ago, 'it gives one werry gentlemanly ideas'.

THE WINES OF CHAMPAGNE

There can be no such list here of AOC and VDQS wines as there are at the end of other chapters. Only three wines of the region are granted *appellation* status: champagne itself, in its sparkling form and in its still, and a pink wine from the outlying Aube region, the champagne of which is not among the best.

Here, though, is a modest dictionary that may help to amplify what has gone before:

Blanc de Blancs

This is not an *appellation*, has no legal validity, and is subject to no checks on its authenticity, so that some cynics say that all that is needed to make it is an instruction to the printer of your labels.

But a few distinguished firms do genuinely make a champagne from white grapes only, and some distinguished critics admire it greatly. Their argument in its favour is something like this: in the typical blend for the classic champagne of must from black and from white grapes, the black grapes give body and fruit, the white grapes delicacy and finesse. Therefore, a wine made from the must of white grapes only will necessarily be *all* delicacy and finesse.

The purists' argument is that the best champagne is a balanced wine because it is a blended wine – above all, because it is blended from black grapes and white.

As in so much else, it is a matter of taste.

BOB

'Buyer's Own Brand', made for clubs, shops and restaurants to sell under their own labels. See page 66.

Bouzy

The still red wine of the region, in which the *champenois* take considerable pride, though it has no *appellation* status. It is light, not unlike a burgundy, but without the depth and with more of the fragrance of sparkling champagne. At most of the hospitable tables of the region champagne is served throughout the meal, but at some Bouzy accompanies the main course: I have often wished for claret.

Champagne

The only *appellation* name that does not need to be accompanied on the label by the words 'appellation contrôlée'. The very name of the wine – the first to be given the status – is held to be enough, just as Great Britain, as the first country to issue adhesive postage stamps, is not required by international law to put its name on them. The word 'champagne' must appear on the cork of every bottle.

Champagne Rosé

Or pink champagne. Like *blanc de blancs*, it is not an *appellation contrôlée*, but the law does lay down how it may be made – by leaving the juice of the black grapes for longer on the skins than usual – though not so long, of course, as for a fully red wine. This is the classic method by which the best still rosés are made, but very few, if any, champagne houses now favour it, as it is difficult to control the colour thus obtained or to be sure of its eventual development in a sparkling wine.

It may also be made by adding to the white wine a proportion of the still red wine of the region – probably from Bouzy – and this, I think, is now the universal practice.

Made even in this latter way, pink champagne is expensive, because the stability of the colour is still uncertain, though less so than when it is obtained by leaving the juice on the skins.

It can still fade in the bottle, or turn a pale tawny, or 'onion-skin' colour.

Now it must not be supposed that, because pink champagne looks pretty and carries overtones of frivolity, it is sweet. It could, of course, be made sweet, as any champagne can be, but by its nature it is fuller-flavoured, harder and drier than the classic golden champagne: it may very well be longer-lived in bottle. Even if it were made sweet, this fullness of flavour would still be there, behind the sweetness, and so could well be the greater staying-power. For, obviously, as it is the juice of the black grape that gives body to the classic wine, there will be more body still if, in addition to the juice, there is an extract from the skins. Also from the skins comes the tannin that gives dryness and staying power to a red wine – astringency, even, until it mellows with age in bottle.

So the *champenois* purist's argument against pink champagne is that although it may be regarded by some as femininely pretty to the eye, it is, in fact, hard and masculine to the taste.

I have heard a *vigneron* say that he always detected 'a taste of gooseberry' in pink champagne, by which, I think, he meant not sourness, but an asperity not found in the traditional golden wine – an element of tannin from the skins of the black grapes. And the director of a *grande marque* house that itself makes a vintage pink champagne, and a good one, has said that the typical maker of the traditional wine of the region, 'considers it alien to the mainstream of its destiny'.

But it is pretty; it is frivolous only to look at; and I like it.

Méthode Champenoise

Not an *appellation* exactly, but the words are protected by law: sparkling wine may be made in other regions, and from the grape appropriate to the region, but the method used in making champagne must be followed exactly – only so many permitted pressings; secondary fermentation in bottle; disgorgement from the bottle after *remuage*; and the rest of it – if a sparkling burgundy, say, or a sparkling Vouvray is to state on its label that it is made by *méthode champenoise*. Otherwise it says merely *vin mousseux* and, if very cheap indeed, will have had the gas pumped into it but, if it is a respectable wine, it will have been made by the *cuve close* method – secondary fermentation in tank, and the sediment got rid of by filtering.

Coteaux Champenois

For a long time, the export of the still white wine of the region was forbidden, lest unprincipled foreigners turned it fraudulently fizzy, and sold it as champagne. Then there was a partial relaxation of the ban, especially in years of big crops: the surplus over what the law permits to be used for sparkling wine was allowed to be sold as still champagne, but not permitted an *appellation*.

It was granted the name – not an *appellation* – *vin natur de la Champagne*, but not 'champagne natur' lest there be misunderstanding. (The word 'champagne' itself is so jealously protected that even the maker of the local mustard is not allowed to state on his label, in any language, that his product is made of mustard and champagne: it has to be *moutarde au vin provenant de la Champagne*: made from 'mustard seed, wine from Champagne district'.)

In 1974 the new *appellation* Coteaux Champenois was created, thus obviating the use of the word champagne itself. The word '*natur*' is not included, because *chaptalisation* is permitted.

The *appellation* applies to the reds and rosés of the region, such as Bouzy and Riceys, and the conditions and restrictions are as severe as those governing the production of the sparkling wine itself.

Moët and Chandon make a still white wine, stylishly

bottled and labelled; there is a Laurent-Perrier; and there has once at any rate been a Bollinger. All these wines are elegant, well-balanced, dry but fruity, and too expensive. They can all now carry the new *appellation* on their labels.

Rosé des Riceys

A pink wine, and the only wine in the region other than champagne itself and Coteaux Champenois with the AOC *appellation*. Made from the Pinot grape in the Aube region, which is outside and cut off from the main Champagne vineyards, though its sparkling wines are entitled to the *appellation*: they are lesser breeds, but within the law. In all the twenty years I have been visiting Champagne, no *champenois* has ever offered me a rosé des Riceys, or even mentioned it. I had never heard of it until I came to write this book, and it is not mentioned in Patrick Forbes's vast classic work. *Appellation* notwithstanding, I cannot believe it has much to say for itself.

*

For Further Reading

FORBES, PATRICK, *Champagne*, Gollancz, 1967.
RAY, CYRIL, *Bollinger*, Peter Davies, 1971.
SIMON, ANDRÉ, *The History of Champagne*, Ebury Press, 1962.

CHAPTER 4

Burgundy

FOR a thousand years, and until a mere five hundred years ago, Burgundy was sometimes a kingdom, more often a duchy, for most of that millennium owing nominal allegiance to, but often at war with, the kingdom of France.

In the period of its greatest political and cultural vigour, which is to say the fifteenth century, Philip the Good (after the death of whose son, Charles the Bold, in 1477, the duchy reverted to the French crown) ruled from his capital, Dijon, a powerful state that included most of what are now Belgium, Luxembourg and the Netherlands, the north-eastern French provinces of Flanders, Artois, Hainault and Picardy, and a vast stretch of territory between the Loire on the west and the mountains of the Jura on the east.

Thus, there is an historical reason for Belgium's and Holland's traditional love for, and knowledge of, fine burgundies, as there is for the English traditional affection for claret.

A later historical link with the Low Countries was forged when many, perhaps most, of the Protestants of the region who were expelled from France by the Revocation of the Edict of Nantes in 1685 fled to Protestant Holland.

The Revolution split the historic provinces of France into *départements*, and as a place-name 'la Bourgogne' has no more official standing in France than 'Wessex', say, in England. (Though we have re-created Cumbria, and the historical regions of Wales.)

Indeed, although any Frenchman of our time knows

whether or not he is Burgundian, just as he knows whether or not he is Provençal or Champenois, even the most self-consciously proud Burgundian would be hard put to it to define the precise boundaries of what he knows in his bones and his blood to be Burgundy.

What he does know, though, and what every other Frenchman and Frenchwoman would agree or, in some cases, grudgingly admit, is that this is the belly of France.

Hence come Charollais beef and the plump, white-fleshed *poulets* and *poulardes* of Bresse; fat snails, the raw ham of Morvan and the marbled, pink-and-green, *jambon persillé*; trout and crayfish and pike and eels; *meurettes*, which are wine sauces, and Dijon mustard; many kinds of fungi and more kinds of game; *pain d'épice*, which is a honey-cake, and *crème de cassis*, which is sweet blackcurrant cordial.

Here, and south as far as Lyons, just outside what we generally regard as Burgundy, but culturally and gastronomically a part of it, are more restaurants regarded as worthy of Guide Michelin stars than any other part of France of similar size.

In those restaurants and with those dishes are served the wines of the region – red wines that are rivalled only by those of Bordeaux as the greatest red wines in the world, and whites that many great amateurs of wine regard as incomparable, though others hold that the great wines of the Rhine and the Mosel can perhaps be mentioned in the same breath.

They are very different, though. Indeed, white burgundy has a style all its own, much more austere, far less flowery, than the wines of Germany or, for that matter, of Alsace, firmer and more, as it were, masculine than those of the Loire, and without the underlying sweetness of even the driest white Bordeaux.

Quite dry, then, yet mellow and full of flavour at its best, white burgundy can be dull and flabby at its meanest. As in

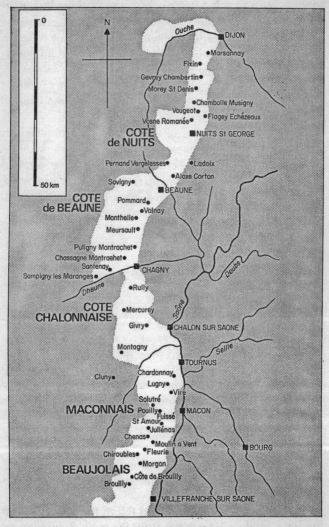

Map 4. Burgundy

most things, one gets what one pays for – and the best of all white burgundies are the dearest of all.

Chiefly, this is because there is very little of them – very little white burgundy at all, in fact, never mind of the finest.

Edmund Penning-Rowsell has pointed out in his *Red, White and Rosé* that Burgundy produces about one-tenth as much red and white wine as Bordeaux: only one-sixth of the total is white, and about one-tenth of that one-sixth is of AOC quality.

Nor is all the AOC white burgundy to be described as 'fine'.

In the main, the wines of Burgundy are grown in small-holdings by peasant-proprietors.

The Burgundian nobility of the Middle Ages was pious – or, it may be, so impious that it was especially concerned about its after-life. Much land went to the Church. These great ecclesiastical estates were split up at the Revolution among the peasants and they have been further fragmented since, by the French law of inheritance, which divides properties equally between all children of the same parents.

In the Bordelais, the great wine-growing estates forfeited by *aristos* who had lost their heads or left the country were bought up by syndicates, by get-rich-quick contractors to the armies of Napoleon or, later, by the financiers of the Second Empire, so that, as Morton Shand observed in *A Book of French Wines*, 'the Bordelais is still a viticultural feudality grouped round the château, which, with its wine-presses, cellars, and extensive vineyards, is nearly always held in single tenancy'.

In Burgundy, on the other hand, the 120 acres of the famous Clos de Vougeot, to take only one example, is split among fifty proprietors and, to confuse the consumer even more, includes some of the best soil of the region and some that is mere run of the mill.

And along with these finest burgundies, red and white, are the less ambitious table wines from the same communes, as well as the modest wines of southern Burgundy, from the regions of Mercurey, the Côte Chalonnaise, the Mâconnais, and especially the Beaujolais.

Let us begin, though, in the north, as we consider in greater detail the lie of this famous land.

By no means the whole – indeed, only a very small part – of what was once the duchy of Burgundy is under vines. Much of the region – 30 per cent of its area – is forest; much is pasture; a good deal is mountain and moor.

The vineyards of Burgundy run in a narrow, broken, strip, from north to south, in the *départements* of Yonne, the Côte d'Or, Saône-et-Loire and Rhône.

In the *département* of the Yonne, the vineyards of Chablis lie around that tiny country town, between Auxerre and Tonnerre, the best of them facing south or south-west on the right bank of the Serein, a tributary of the Yonne, itself a tributary of the Seine.

Dry and pale, typically a wine of the north, true Chablis has a springtime smell and a clean, crisp, freshness: it goes particularly well with oysters. Alas, production is small, and the wine is much imitated, in 'Chablis-type' wines from countries where the sun is too hot for a wine so delicate as the real Chablis to be produced: its reputation has suffered unfairly.

The Chablis vineyards form a little island, so to speak, of their own: it is ninety miles or so from Chablis south-east to Dijon, and that is where the rest of the great Burgundy vineyards begin – the long, narrow slope of the Côte d'Or, so-called not, as most people suppose, because it is a golden slope, but because it faces east – the Orient.

The northern stretch of the Côte d'Or is the Côte de Nuits, named after the little country town (now hyphenated into Nuits-Saint-Georges, in honour of the great vineyards of Les Saint-Georges) – a twelve-mile stretch, sometimes half-a-mile wide, sometimes a mere couple of hundred yards, of hillside vineyards, facing east, producing almost entirely red wines.

In spite of the strong family resemblance between all red burgundies, these are generally rather fuller than those of the Côte de Beaune, slower to mature and, therefore, longer-lasting – though no burgundies take so long to reach or to pass their best as the great clarets.

This may well be the point to make the comparison that every writer about French wines has to make, between claret and red burgundy – the wines not only by which all the other red wines in the world are judged, but each of which serves as a standard of comparison for the other.

Just as there are Manchester United men and Manchester City men, Oxford men and Cambridge men, Sotheby's men and Christie's men, Lafite men and Mouton men – by which I mean not alumni or employees or producers or players, but advocates, admirers, supporters or customers – so there are burgundy men and claret men.

And the fact that there are such is as much a measure of similarity as of difference: feelings would not run so high, arguments not become so heated, if differences were such as to provide no material for debate. The fallings-out are over fine points.

The real point is that claret and burgundy are similar wines – so similar that some clarets (especially St Emilions and Pomerols) can be taken for burgundies, some burgundies (especially from the Côte de Beaune) for clarets.

A former colleague of mine, the late and much-lamented Denzil Batchelor, once sought to clinch an argument on this very topic by appealing to Harry Waugh, one of the trade's most experienced, knowledgeable and highly respected tasters:

'Have you ever mistaken a claret for a burgundy, Harry?' asked Denzil.

'Not since luncheon,' said Harry, wryly.

There are differences, of course, and many writers about wine – I have been one of them myself, racking my brains for some magazine article – have sought to express and to simplify them by recommending that the lighter, more subtle, more delicate claret is to drink with grills and roasts and cold meats; the heartier, fuller, more robust burgundy with game and with rich stews.

This is all nonsense, and I say so with authority because I have myself been guilty of perpetrating it. Burgundy will go with any dish that claret will go with, and claret with the richest of meats. It is a matter of taste.

And as for the French saying that burgundy is 'the king of wines', because of its alleged 'bigness', claret 'the queen', because of its delicacy, this too is to exaggerate a difference. It would be just as near the mark – to my mind, it would be nearer – to describe burgundy as the more feminine wine of the two because, in so far as it is different from claret, it is rather softer, rather rounder, rather sweeter, matures earlier, and I would add, were I an anti-feminist, which I am not, because it is less reliable.

If most women, in the western world and in the twentieth century, *are* on the whole less reliable than most men, it is not because of any inherent difference between the sexes, but because most women have not yet been vouchsafed the education, the training and the responsibility of most men. If burgundy is less reliable than claret, it is not because of an inherent difference in the wines but because, as I have already pointed out, it is produced from tiny properties by peasant owners. A vineyard with a great name may be split between a score or more of owners: one has the strip that catches the sun, one has a patch that does not, or that drains badly. One owner is a conscientious tender of his vines, another is content to make a living out of the name on the label of his bottle and is careless about its contents. Few of them have the presses, the casks and the vats to make and mature their own wine, but sell to a shipper, direct or through a middleman, the shipper doing the bottling.

There *are* domaine-bottled burgundies: they are to be preferred to generic blends. In the region itself, the best shippers know which growers to trust; in importing countries such as Britain it is good to know which shippers to trust. There is a short and by no means exhaustive list at the end of this chapter of outstanding shippers of good burgundies.

*

This digression has filled the gap between the two stretches of the Côte d'Or – the break in the escarpment after the Côte de Nuits, near the village of Comblanchien and its great quarries. After this comes the Côte de Beaune, named after the picturesque town, continuing for about fifteen miles the eastward and south-eastward-facing strip of hillside vineyards. It is twice the area of the Côte de Nuits, in most places a good deal wider, and producing such great white burgundies as Montrachet and Meursault as well as reds which, generally speaking, are softer and more delicate than – though few are quite so noble as – their brothers of the Côte de Nuits.

Before leaving the Côte d'Or, there are a couple of points to be made about its wines.

The matter of nomenclature is one: it is well to remember that many communes (villages, we would call them, or even rural districts) have hyphenated their names with that of their most illustrious vineyards. Thus Chassagne-Montrachet is a commune wine. So the single-barrelled name is more aristocratic than the double-barrelled. So, too, with Vosne-Romanée and the various Romanée vineyards, with Gevrey-Chambertin inferior to Chambertin, and so on.

Then *chaptalisation* – the process of adding sugar to the

grape-must, to assist fermentation when there is not enough natural sugar in the grapes: this is always permitted in Burgundy, under strict control of course, whereas it is permitted only exceptionally in Bordeaux, which is farther south and does not have the same problem, or has it only in particularly poor years. The added sugar does not make the wine sweeter, as it all ferments out. In so far as burgundy can be described as being sweeter than claret – perhaps it is generally softer and fruitier rather than actually sweeter – this is because of grape and soil, *not* the added sugar.

South of the two fine-wine regions, Côte de Beaune and Côte de Nuits, that together make up the great Côte d'Or, are three distinct areas the wines of which are sometimes classed together, in wine-merchants' and restaurant lists, under the heading 'Southern Burgundy', to distinguish them from the classic reds and whites of the Côte d'Or and Chablis.

There is some justice in this: none of their wines is in the same class as the finest of its northern neighbours. But much wine is grown in these southern districts, and it has given, and gives, much pleasure.

There are pleasant, light-bodied red wines, for instance, from the Côte Chalonnaise or the Chalonnais, an area that runs almost without a break into the Mâconnais, whence come both reds and whites, among the latter the delightful and quite reasonably distinguished Pouilly-Fuissé, in which Philip Youngman Carter detected 'the fragrance of young nuts dipped in melon' – as far-fetched a comparison as I have come across in recent writing about wine. It has something of the fullness of flavour of a Côte de Beaune white, something of the crisp cleanness of a Loire.

The southern end of the Mâconnais and the northern of the Beaujolais overlap, and there is some permitted choice of *appellations* for the whites and for a very few reds (see list, below).

Considering the popularity of the wine itself, its very name whispering to English ears intimations of personability and of pleasure, and considering the popularity of Chevallier's up-roariously ribald novel *Clochemerle*, which is set in these parts, the Beaujolais is remarkably little visited.

It is delightfully rolling, wooded country, from the high hills of which one can see the Jura and even, when the weather is propitious, Alpine peaks. Its villages – even that which claims to be the true Clochemerle – are modest, with simple little bistros, and shabby little cafés at which to drink the local wine by the glass. It is cheap, and it is served without pretension or chi-chi.

Rightly so, for Beaujolais is, as John Arlott has put it, 'the drinking man's wine . . . the best of all tippling wines'.

Made from the Gamay grape, which is not regarded as 'noble' in Burgundy, Beaujolais is meant to be drunk young and cool, when it is both fresh and refreshing (again to quote John Arlott, 'the only wine that truly quenches the thirst – virtually all other alcoholic drinks simply increase it').

There are a few exceptions to this generalization of drinking Beaujolais young and cool. The *grand crus** – those wines entitled to their individual names as *appellations* – such as Brouilly, Chénas, Chiroubles, Côte de Brouilly, Fleurie, Juliénas, Morgon, Moulin-à-Vent and Saint Amour, are made like burgundies, to be matured in bottle, and some of them – Morgon and Moulin-à-Vent especially – will age for as long as a good example of the Côte de Nuits.

Because a great deal of Beaujolais is made to be drunk

---

* A *cru* is the precise piece of land on which a particular wine is grown and, by extension, the wine itself. It is translated into English as 'growth'. It is sometimes applied to a particularly fine single-vineyard wine within an *appellation* area: the finest clarets, for instance, are each referred to as a *cru* (see Chapter 10). In Burgundy, another word for it is *climat*.

virtually as soon as it has fermented from must into being wine, and because in Lyons and then in Paris it became a matter of pride to bistros that sold cheap, refreshing wine to offer young Beaujolais by the glass as soon as it was ready, a great cult developed of drinking not merely young Beaujolais, but the youngest.

There are races now, using aeroplanes and racing cars, to be the first London shipper or restaurant or wine club to have the *Beaujolais primeur* on offer by 14 November of the vintage year, the first date permitted by French law; *Beaujolais nouveau* may be sold as such on 15 December (too late for gimmickry – the *Beaujolais primeur* has stolen all the thunder by then) and until the next vintage; and *Beaujolais de l'année* may be sold as such until the second month of March after the vintage – until the next year's wine is in the shops, that is.

Beaujolais must be specially made if it is to be drunk as young as this – only the shortest possible time on the skins and in wood – and so it goes over the hill very quickly: it has no staying-power. The cult for drinking it very young has been grossly overdone, save that there is something to be said for anything that shows the wine-drinking public that age in wine is not always, and in every instance, a virtue.

Some white Beaujolais is made – not very much, and not much to my liking. It has a coarseness that is part of the fruitiness of the red wine of the region, but that is unbecoming in a white.

THE WINES OF BURGUNDY

All the wines in this list are AOC.

Aloxe-Corton

The name of the town, at the northern end of the Côte de Beaune, is Aloxe (pronounced 'Aloss'); it hyphenates that of its most famous vineyard, so that a Corton, *tout simple*, is more aristocratic than an Aloxe-Corton.

There are very few whites, and the finest (such as Corton-Charlemagne) have *appellations* of their own.

The *appellation* followed by the words 'premier cru' or the name of a specific *climat* (vineyard) indicates higher quality within the commune *appellation*. But, as always with burgundies, it is the shipper that counts. In general, the red wines of this commune are firmer than other Beaunes, and live longer. The ordinary whites, as distinct from the Corton-Charlemagne, are run of the mill.

Auxey-Duresses
A small *appellation* in the Côte de Beaune, mostly good, typical Beaune reds, and a few less remarkable whites.

Bâtard-Montrachet
One of the very greatest of the great white wines of the Côte de Beaune – 'barely perceptibly inferior', wrote Morton Shand, 'to the great Le Montrachet itself'. Deep in flavour, with a pronounced flowery bouquet.

Beaujolais
Beaujolais Supérieur
Beaujolais Villages
The virtues of this very easily drinkable wine are touched upon in pages 83–4.

It must be made from the Gamay *noir à jus blanc*, and the Supérieur and the Villages are each a cut above the simple *appellation*. Beaujolais Supérieur and Beaujolais Villages must reach a minimum of 10 degrees alcohol as against the Beaujolais 9, and Beaujolais Villages can come only from one or more of thirty-nine named communes – the best of which, though, have individual *appellations* of their own.

There is about one-tenth as much white as red Beaujolais: it has to reach a minimum of 0·5 degree of alcohol stronger than the red.

Beaune

The lowest *appellation* for the reds and the white of the Côte de Beaune – the reds a little softer than those of the Côte de Nuits; the whites, even with the simple *appellation*, often very good indeed.

The name followed by '*premier cru*', or bracketed with one of the *premier crus* – for example, Beaune les Marconnets – or with one of the single vineyards of one of these *crus* – for example, Beaune-Grèves de l'Enfant Jesus will indicate higher quality as well as greater alcoholic strength and longer life.

Bienvenues Bâtard-Montrachet

The smallest of the white *grands crus* of the Montrachet area. H. W. Yoxall ranks it only just below Le Montrachet itself and a photo-finish margin ahead of Bâtard-Montrachet (see above). Yet Morton Shand, dithyrambic about the Montrachet, its bastard brother and Chevalier-Montrachet, mentions it not at all!

In any case, a great wine, and appropriately expensive, for its acreage is only one-fifth that of Bâtard-Montrachet, and one-thirtieth of Le Montrachet.

Blagny

Red wines from the Puligny–Montrachet district – not often met with, but worth looking out for on or near their home ground. They have the softness and suppleness of the best Beaunes, and have seemed to me, on the rare occasions I have come across them, to be more beguiling to the nose than most.

The white wines are entitled to be styled Meursault-Blagny (q.v.).

Bonnes Mares

A *premier cru* of Chambolle-Musigny (q.v.) and one of the greatest reds of the Côte de Nuits, from a vineyard (once convent-owned, it is said, and originally 'Bonnes Mères', though Morton Shand derives the name from an Old French verb, *marer*, to tend vines). It is under more than one ownership, so that some bottles are better than others. At its best, though, a big, round, smooth wine with gradations of delicacy behind its bold front, and a greater capacity for ageing than most burgundies.

Bourgogne
Bourgogne Aligoté
Bourgogne Clairet
Bourgogne Rosé
Bourgogne Ordinaire or Bourgogne Grand Ordinaire
Bourgogne Ordinaire or
   Bourgogne Grand Ordinaire Clairet
Bourgogne Ordinaire or
   Bourgogne Grand Ordinaire Rosé

It would be absurd to try to distinguish too minutely between these seven *appellations*. '*Bourgogne*' is the *appellation* for the reds and whites of the region. Only certain grapes are permitted but they may be blended, and wine from different communes may also be blended, so long as they are within the officially delimited Burgundy region.

I do not know of any difference between '*clairet*' and '*rosé*', but it is worth noting that the simple *appellation* '*Bourgogne*' outranks the '*ordinaire*' and the '*grand ordinaire*'.

The Aligoté grape is inferior to the noble Chardonnay, but a good Bourgogne Aligoté is a very pleasant table wine in the restaurants of the region: I fancy that the best may have an admixture of Chardonnay, though still entitled only to the inferior *appellation*.

Bourgogne Hautes Côtes de Beaune
Bourgogne Clairet Hautes Côtes de Beaune
Bourgogne Rosé Hautes Côtes de Beaune
Bourgogne Hautes Côtes de Nuits
Bourgogne Clairet Hautes Côtes de Nuits
Bourgogne Rosé Hautes Côtes de Nuits
See the previous entry: '*clairet*' and '*rosé*' are the same thing. The other *appellations* cover reds and whites from certain communes in the two côtes, and only after tasting by an official panel. Usually a shade finer, therefore, than plain burgundies or, at any rate, a shade more expensive.

Bourgogne Marsannay or Bourgogne Marsannay la Côte
Quite one of the best rosés of the region, from the outskirts of Dijon.

Bourgogne Passetoutgrains
Reds and rosés made from one-third of the classic Pinot grape, two-thirds of the Gamay *noir au jus Blanc* which, except in the Beaujolais, is not regarded as a 'noble' grape. These reds and pinks are the equivalent in quality and esteem of the Bourgogne Aligoté white – good, sound carafe wines, but not for special seeking out.

Bourgogne Mousseux
Red, white and rosé burgundies can be made to sparkle, and if this is done by the *méthode champenoise* it may be called 'Bourgogne Mousseux'. There are better sparkling whites and rosés, and not only from Champagne. I cannot remember when I last drank a sparkling red burgundy, but what I do remember is that I didn't like it.

Brouilly
One of the nine '*crus*' of Beaujolais, and the biggest. Not a

common wine to be drunk *very* young, but does mature quickly, and is probably at its best after two or three years.

Chablis
Chablis Grand Cru
Chablis Premier Cru
Petit Chablis

For style and quality, see pages 75–8.

White wines only, and only from the Chardonnay, the grand cru comes from a severely limited area, just by the town of Chablis itself, must be at least 11 degrees, and yield per acre is more limited than that for the other *appellations*.

Chablis premier cru may be followed by the name of one of a number of named *climats*: it is permitted a higher yield per acre and 0·5 degrees less alcohol.

Chablis must be 10 degrees, and Petit Chablis 9·5.

Chambertin
Chambertin-Clos-de-Bèze

Two of the eight red *grands crus* of the Gevrey–Chambertin commune at the northern end of the Côte de Nuits and generally regarded as the greatest.

The seventy acres covered by the two are split up among a couple of dozen proprietors. There is little to choose between Chambertin and Chambertin-Clos-de-Bèze; more difference between the different proprietors and shippers. When at their best, the two wines are immensely deep in colour and in smell – 'vigorous, militant wines', H. W. Yoxall calls them.

One might suppose that this is why Chambertin was Napoleon's favourite wine until one learns that he used to water it.

Chambolle-Musigny

The greatest growths of this commune in the middle of the

Côte de Nuits have *appellations* of their own: Musigny and Bonnes Mares. The name of the village, Chambolle, hyphenated with that of its most famous growth, is a general *appellation*, but it can be styled '*premier cru*' if it comes from one of twenty named *climats*, or it can hyphenate the name of any of them.

According to French commentators on the region, 'the most scented, fine and delicate of the whole of the Côte de Nuits'. Certainly, even Chambolle-Musigny, *tout court*, without any *cru* or *climat* mentioned, can be a most winningly soft and scented wine.

Chapelle-Chambertin

The biggest in vineyard area of the eight great reds of Gevrey-Chambertin that rank after Chambertin and Chambertin-Clos-de-Bèze (qq.v.) in the hierarchy of *grands crus*, and do not need to bear the hyphenated commune name: they hyphenate their own name with that of Chambertin itself.

Charlemagne

An *appellation* accorded to a white wine, related to Corton-Charlemagne, that seems to have gone out of production.

Charmes-Chambertin

Another of the eight great reds of Gevrey–Chambertin. See under Chapelle-Chambertin.

Chassagne-Montrachet

The commune whence come some of the greatest white burgundies – Montrachet and its near relatives (qq.v.). In the commune generally, some very good red wines are also produced. The best whites are dry though rich in fruit and flavour but, as everywhere else in Burgundy, there is considerable variation in quality.

Cheilly-les-Maranges
An *appellation* of Santenay (q.v.): it is little met with.

Chénas
Smallest of the nine *crus* of Beaujolais, not ranked so high as
Moulin-à-Vent or Fleurie, and sometimes seems to have a
sharp edge to it. Can be charming, though, drunk within a
couple of years of the vintage.

Chevalier-Montrachet
Ranks with Bâtard-Montrachet and Bienvenues-Bâtard-
Montrachet (qq.v.).

Chiroubles
One of the smaller of the nine *crus* of the Beaujolais, and
perhaps one of the fruitier. But the differences between eight
of the nine are slight – the odd man out, because biggest and
best, is Moulin-à-Vent (q.v.).

Chorey-lès-Beaune
A red wine from one of the villages entitled to the *appellation*
Côte-de-Beaune-Villages (q.v.) or to its own name, simply.

Clos-de-la-Roche
One of the four *grands crus* of Morey-St-Denis, along with
Bonnes Mares (partly in Chambolle-Musigny), Clos-de-Tart,
and Clos-St-Denis: pretty full, strapping wine, not so well-
known as some, and yet showing the bigness that many
people look for in a burgundy.

Clos-de-Tart
See above. This is one of the four mentioned that is under
single ownership, and is therefore more consistent than the

others: 'a lovely, soft, strong and savoury wine', in Hugh Johnson's opinion,* and all the more desirable in that it matures early and so can be drunk young, when full of fruit, yet lives long, developing more subtlety than most wines of that sort.

Clos-de-Vougeot

The 125 acres of vineyards enclosed in a vast stone wall, with the great eleventh-century Cistercian press-house looming over it all like a castle, lies hard by Chambolle-Musigny, in the very middle of the Côte de Nuits.

As it is split up among some fifty or sixty proprietors, some with no more than half an acre of vines apiece, and as the quality of the separate wines varies according to whether it comes from the sun-facing upper slopes, or from the flat land at the bottom, it is impossible to be whole-hearted.

Certainly not so whole-hearted as Colonel Brisson, of the Revolutionary Army of the Rhine, who bade his regiment halt at the *clos* and present arms, which the French Army, I am told, does to this day.

(I have never understood why writers have attributed the *beau geste* to Napoleon, to the Duc d'Aumale, to Marshal MacMahon, or to officers unknown: the story is told by Stendhal – a great burgundy-lover – who soldiered with Bisson's contemporaries, and could well have had the story first-hand or, at any rate, when it was well within living memory.)

The finest Clos-de-Vougeot, from the *climats* on the upper slopes, is lighter and drier than most of its peers and is sometimes described as being more like a claret, just as the fatter Pomerols and St Emilions are likened to burgundies.

Hugh Johnson credits it with 'the most beautiful scent in

*Hugh Johnson, *Wine* (Nelson, 1966).

Burgundy', but 'with a faint suggestion of autumnal dankness about it which is typically burgundian'.*

The great building, much restored, is used for bacchanalian bean-feasts by the Chevaliers du Tastevin, a mock-medieval fraternity founded in the nineteen-thirties to promote burgundy and the profits of its growers. The pattern has been followed in every wine-growing area in France, particularly since the war. (I think the Jurade of St Emilion is the only confraternity of its kind that has an unbroken history going back to the Middle Ages.)

Clos-Saint-Denis

Along with Clos-de-la-Roche and Clos-de-Tart (qq.v.) one of the *grands crus* of Morey-St-Denis: like the others, a big wine with 'plenty of stuffing', to quote a French admirer.

Corton

See under Aloxe-Corton, of which Le Corton is the great red wine – perhaps the greatest of the Beaune reds. It needs more bottle-age than most and then develops a brilliance of colour, a velvety texture and a deep violet-like smell that together are enchanting.

There is a very little white Corton, but the great white wine of the name is Corton-Charlemagne, below.

Corton-Charlemagne

So-named because the great emperor owned all the vineyards round here until he gave them to the Church.

Ranks with Meursault and Montrachet as one of the greatest white burgundies, but with perhaps a little more backbone: it has body enough to go with the richest food.

*Hugh Johnson, *Wine* (Nelson, 1966).

Côte de Beaune

Commune wines from the general area, mostly red, but a little white entitled to the *appellation* is produced. Good, wholesome wines, quick to mature, still relatively inexpensive and (although I prefer good claret to good burgundy) I must add that they are usually better value than Bordeaux wines of the same price.

Côte de Beaune-Villages

All these wines are red; other things being equal, which they never are in the world of wine, they could be assumed to be slightly better-bred than a Côte de Beaune.

They come from the following *communes*, which are also entitled to bracket their names with either of these two *appellations*:

Auxey-Duresses	Monthelié
Blagny	Pernand-Vergelesses
Chassagne-Montrachet	Puligny-Montrachet
Cheilly-lès-Maranges	Saint-Aubin
Chorey-lès-Beaune	Sampigny-lès-Maranges
Dezize-lès-Maranges	Santenay
Ladoix	Savigny-lès-Beaune
Meursault	

Côte de Brouilly

One of the nine *communes* of the Beaujolais entitled to an individual *appellation*: from a very much smaller area than Brouilly (q.v.) and regarded as usually marginally its superior.

Côte de Nuits-Villages

There is no simple Côte de Nuits *appellation*, as there is a Côte de Beaune distinct from a Côte de Beaune-Villlages. Five communes only – Fixin, Brochon, Prissey, Comblanchien and

Corgoloin – are entitled to sell under this name as well as their own. The wines are virtually all red, harder and more 'masculine' than wines of comparable quality from the Côte de Beaune.

Criots Bâtard-Montrachet
A splendid white wine, the peer of Bâtard-Montrachet and Bienvenus-Montrachet (qq.v.).

Dezize-lès-Maranges
See under Côte de Beaune-Villages.

Echézaux
Quite the largest of the seven great growths of Vosne-Romanée:

Romanée-Conti	Romanée-St-Vivant
Richebourg	Grands-Echézaux
Romanée	Echézaux
La Tâche	

Of these the Domaine de la Romanée-Conti owns the vineyard of that name, together with La Tâche, part of Richebourg and part of Grands-Échézaux.

Scholars of wine, used to drinking and comparing the very greatest, can find subtle differences between these noble wines: I cannot.

As dry red wines go, they are deep in flavour and smoothly luscious, almost spicy: 'at once velvet and satin', is a phrase about them that is much-quoted.

It is often hinted, sometimes boldly asserted, about the Domaine's wines that, to quote H. W. Yoxall, 'there must be some secret of vinification, apart from the merits of the vineyards'[*] or, in Hugh Johnson's words, 'whispers about adding

[*] H. W. Yoxall, *The Wines of Burgundy* (Penguin, 1974).

a touch of brandy, or concentrating a small proportion of the unfermented juice'.*

However that may be, the result is a majesty of colour, body and fragrance and, needless to say, correspondingly majestic prices. There are fewer bottles of these wines each year than of the great first-growths of Bordeaux, and they are harder to come by, for love or for money.

Chambertin and Chambertin-Clos-de-Bèze are the only other burgundies in anything like the same class.

Fixin
See under Côte de Nuits-Villages.

Fleurie
One of the nine individually-named *communes* of the Beaujolais, Fleurie is one of the biggest and most popular – lighter than Moulin-à-Vent and, according to Alexis Lichine, the most typical of Beaujolais in its fresh fruitiness.

Gevrey-Chambertin
Red wine from the *commune* of which Chambertin and Clos-de-Bèze are the glories. A couple of dozen *climats* can hyphenate their names with the already hyphenated name.

This is one of the most reliable of generic *appellations*: a Gevrey-Chambertin from a reliable supplier is likely to be a generous wine, full of character.

Givry
From the Chalonnais, between the Côte d'Or and the Maconnais (south of which again is the Beaujolais). Both whites and reds, mostly reds, which are not unlike Beaunes in style and quality and, now that the better-known names of burgundy are so expensive, very good value.

*Hugh Johnson, *Wine* (Nelson, 1966).

Grands Échézaux
See under Échézaux.

Griotte Chambertin
One of the *grands crus* of Gevrey-Chambertin (q.v.) and a
fine example of its well-bred heartiness.

Juliénas
Pronounce the final 's' in the name of this one of nine
Beaujolais communes. Not perhaps so immediately appealing
as Fleurie, but those Juliénas that reach Britain, having been
specially selected by British shippers on the spot, and then
given a couple of years' bottle-age, can be remarkably handsome, forthcoming red table wines.

Ladoix
See under Côte de Beaune-Villages.

Latricières-Chambertin
One of the '*premiers crus*' of Gevrey-Chambertin (q.v.).

Mâcon
Mâcon-Supérieur
Mâcon-Villages
The Mâconnais, between the Chalonnais and the Beaujolais,
produces reds and rosés, from the Gamay or the Pinot, and
whites, which may hyphenate their name with the *appellation*
Pinot-Chardonnay if made from that grape (usually called in
Burgundy, and more correctly, simply Chardonnay).

Pouilly-Fuissé and a couple of other Mâcon whites enjoy
appellations of their own; white Mâcon-Villages and Mâcon-
Supérieur are often sold simply as white burgundies.

Mâcon-Villages is an *appellation* for white wines only; the
difference between Mâcon and Mâcon Supérieur is of one
degree alcohol only.

Mâcon may be hyphenated with the name of some nearly forty *communes*, too many to be listed here, though Mâcon-Viré can be mentioned as a sound white now becoming well-known in Britain.

MM. Poupon and Forgeot make the point in their *The Wines of Burgundy* that the Mâconnais was the boundary between the *langue d'oc* of the south and the *langue d'oil* of the north (see page 133), and that it is here that the Pinot gives way to the Gamay grape.

Certainly, the climate here is more southern than is that of the Côte d'Or – the summers are hotter, the winters milder. It is for this reason, suggests H. W. Yoxall, that in 'off' years a sound Mâcon is better value than a Côte d'Or burgundy.

Mazis-Chambertin
One of the *grands crus* of Gevrey-Chambertin, a sort of younger cousin of Chambertin itself.

Mazoyères-Chambertin
Another name for Charmes-Chambertin (q.v.).

Mercurey
The best red wine of the Chalonnais (there is only a little white) not unlike good generic Beaune or Côte de Beaune-Villages, deep in colour but lighter in body and texture.

Meursault
'Soft, smooth and scented', says Hugh Johnson of this great white burgundy – never perhaps so great as the greatest Montrachet but a classic example of what a fine wine ought to be – dry without being austere. High in alcohol, with a hint of green in the golden colour and (some say) a taste of hazelnuts.

There are eighteen *premier crus* vineyards, entitled to

bracket their names, of which Les Perrières, Les Charmes and La Goutte d'Or have come my way, and much to my advantage.

Meursault-Blagny

As the best *climats* around Blagny are allowed to style themselves either 'Meursault' or 'Meursault-Blagny', the latter is rarely met with.

Montagny

Sound, forceful white wine from the Chalonnais, near Givry, the reds of which have already been listed.

Monthélie

Good, medium-quality reds from near Volnay, and of the same style – not well-known abroad and particularly well worth looking for in the district restaurants.

Montrachet

Perhaps the greatest dry white wine of France, as Yquem is the greatest sweet wine, though Morton Shand compared the two to Yquem's detriment:

'The wonderful flavour of Château d'Yquem is soon drowned in the syrupy flood of unfermented grape-sugar, while Montrachet is rich and luscious as it is vast and grand from the first sip to the last reflex of after-taste, but without a trace of cloying sweetness ...'

This, though, is to compare unlikes – a dessert with a table wine. Suffice it to say that, for a dry wine, Montrachet is remarkably round and mouth-filling, flowery to the nose, and with depth upon depth of under-flavours.

Not, perhaps, as Alexandre Dumas is said to have counselled, to be drunk kneeling, with bared head – not kneeling, anyway – but certainly to be treated with great respect and drunk with gratitude to Mother Nature and the men who help her.

Morey-Saint-Denis

Red wines from the commune (between Gevrey-Chambertin and Chambolle-Musigny, in the Côte de Nuits) that produces Bonnes-Mares, Clos-Saint-Denis, Clos-de-la-Roche and Clos-de-Tart (qq.v.). A couple of dozen lesser *climats* produce wines very similar in style, much to be recommended.

Morgon

One of the Beaujolais nine, and one of the fuller-bodied.

Moulin-à-Vent

The biggest in body and the best of the nine major *crus* of the Beaujolais, nearest in style to the red burgundies of the Côte d'Or, and well worth four or five years of bottle-age.

Musigny

The *grand cru climat* of twenty-five acres is split among ten owners, so there are variations in quality. But Le Musigny is a fine, smooth red burgundy, deservedly commanding high prices. Bonnes Mares (q.v.) lies partly within the commune.

Nuits or Nuits-St-Georges

The lowest *appellation* for the wines (all red) of the Côte de Nuits: some thirty-five *premier cru climats* can hyphenate their names.

The wines are rather firmer than those of the Côte de Beaune.

Pernand-Vergelesses

Red wines from the northern tip of the Côte de Beaune and near neighbours of Corton, to the wines of which they bear a family resemblance.

Pinot-Chardonnay Mâcon
See under Mâcon.

Pommard
Between Beaune and Volnay, one of the best-known of the
commune names of Burgundy, much abused in the past.

Now that A O C and E E C regulations are so much stricter, one
has the right to expect respectable red wine, rather light as
burgundies go, though Youngman Carter found it 'full-
blooded and firm, a man's drink'* – H.W. Yoxall, on the
other hand, thought it 'without much authority'.

The commune has a couple of dozen named *crus*: I have
drunk very old Les Epenots from among them and found it
delicious.

Pouilly-Fuissé
Pouilly-Loché
Pouilly-Vinzelles
I have referred to Pouilly-Fuissé earlier in this chapter. I hope,
by the way, that no one will confuse it with Pouilly-Fumé,
from the Loire.

In effect, a high-grade white Mâcon, for which the Chardonnay grape is obligatory. Pouilly-Loché and Pouilly-
Vinzelles come from communes adjacent to the twins, Pouilly
and Fuissé; are subject to precisely the same regulations; and to
my palate are indistinguishable from each other and from their
neighbour – greenish-gold, crisp and fresh, with more to
offer the nose than Chablis.

Puligny-Montrachet
The *appellation* for wines of the *commune* that includes such
great white wines as Le Montrachet (q.v.). Puligny-Mon-
trachet whites are the less noble relatives, but they can show

*Youngman Carter, *Drinking Burgundy* (Hamish Hamilton, 1966).

a similar, if not quite so immense, depth of flavour. There are some modest reds also entitled to the name.

Richebourg
Romanée
Romanée-Conti
Romanée-St Vivant
Among the greatest of the Vosne-Romanée wines: see under Échézaux.

Ruchottes-Chambertin
A *grand cru* of Gevrey-Chambertin, entitled to omit the 'Gevrey'. A big wine, like Chambertin itself (q.v.).

Rully
The red Rully, from the Chalonnais, is similar to Givry and to Mercurey (qq.v.); there is more white, which is good local drinking, though much of it goes to make sparkling burgundy.

Saint-Amour
One of the smallest of the nine named Beaujolais *communes* – a very pretty, soft wine, to drink fairly young and fresh, but not *de l'année*.

Saint-Aubin
Reds and whites from near Blagny and Montrachet, rather overshadowed by their grand neighbours.

Saint-Romain
A small *commune* near Auxey-Duresses (q.v., for the same comments apply).

Saint-Véran
A fairly recent *appellation*: in effect this white wine from the

Mâconnais is the same as a Pouilly-Fuissé (q.v.): it observes the same regulations and it tastes the same.

Sampigny-lès-Maranges

Red and white wines from the almost southernmost end of the Côte de Beaune and, therefore, of the Côte d'Or. I cannot remember ever having seen, let alone tasted, a bottle: I think most of the wine grown here is sold as Beaune or Côte de Beaune-Villages simply.

Santenay

Mostly reds, from next door to the above, and thus at the *very* end of the Côte. Nothing outstanding here, but some very drinkable *premiers crus*, notably the Les Gravières, sometimes found in British wine-lists, and usually modestly priced.

Sauvignon-de-St-Bris

A white wine from around a little village near Chablis, but – as the name denotes – from a different grape, that of the Loire rather than of Burgundy. Very light and delicate, like a refined Muscadet and seldom met outside its own area.

Savigny or Savigny-lès-Beaune

From near the town of Beaune itself: the wines are very similar.

La Tâche

See under Echézaux.

Vin du Lyonnais or Coteaux du Lyonnais

I know nothing of these red, white and rosé wines; did not know they existed until I saw them in the list; and cannot find them in any work of reference. It is clear where they come from, and that it is a generic name.

Volnay

Red wines similar to, but according to H. W. Yoxall more interesting than those of next-door Pommard. There are some couple of dozen outstanding *premiers crus*, notably Les Santenots and, Youngman Carter's recommendation, Les Caillerets.

Volnay wines generally are lighter in colour than many burgundies, and mature quickly, so that they *should* be cheaper than some . . .

Very easy wine to drink, and pretty to smell.

Volnay-Santenots

See above.

Vosne-Romanée

The *commune* from which come the seven famous *grands crus* listed under Echézaux. Besides these are ten *premiers crus*, of which I have much admired Malconsorts and Suchots, which hyphenate their names with that of the *commune*. But even the *commune* wines here are well above even burgundy average: H. W. Yoxall advises giving them plenty of bottle-age, and Youngman Carter was unstinting in his praise.

Vougeot

The *appellation* of which the *grand cru* Clos-de-Vougeot (q.v.) is the inner, more restricted and grander: Vougeot may be a degree less in alcohol and a higher yield to the acre. All the same, the area of the *commune* is small and, although much split up, its wines reach a high average of quality. Among its *premier crus* is a small vineyard, La Vigne Blanche, that makes a full-flavoured white *appellation* wine from the Chardonnay, Le Clos Blanc de Vougeot, very like a Meursault – very agreeable, says Youngman Carter, with cold salmon, or with cheese and celery.

Some Recommended Burgundy Shippers

This list cannot be exhaustive: there are a couple of hundred Burgundy shippers. The following few are well-known and respected in Britain (non-inclusion is not an implied criticism):

Bouchard Père et Fils	Louis Jadot
Calvet	Louis Latour
Chanson	Piat (Beaujolais)
Drouhin	Thorin (Beaujolais)

Any good merchant is likely to stock wines from one or more of these firms, or be able to tell you where to find them.

For Further Reading

CARTER, YOUNGMAN, *Drinking Burgundy*, Hamish Hamilton, 1966.

POUPON, PIERRE, and FORGEOT, PIERRE, *The Wines of Burgundy* (English edition), Presses Universitaires de France, Paris, 1971.

YOXALL, H. W., *The Wines of Burgundy*, Penguin, 1974.

CHAPTER 5

The Jura and Savoy

Two beautiful mountain regions of France, each close to the frontier with Switzerland, produce interesting wines that outside their own districts are more read about than drunk, for the wine-growing areas are small, and production, therefore, modest.

Savoy is Brillat-Savarin country: the author of *La Physiologie du Gout* was born, in 1755, in Belley, of which little country town (it lies between Seyssel, where the sparkling wine comes from, and Chambéry, famous for its vermouth) he became mayor.

It was a relative of his, and a contemporary, Lucien Tendret, who wrote of the wines of this splendid region of lakes, rivers and alps that 'if they lack the bouquet of the great wines of Burgundy and Bordeaux, they still have a delightful aroma and leave the mouth fresh and the head clear'.

This is as true now of the white wines of Savoy – and most of the wines of Savoy are white – as it was two hundred years ago, though they are no longer made, as they were in Tendret's time, to 'take longer to grow old than ourselves'. (But that was perhaps a reference to local red wines, which are few, now, and unremarkable.) Indeed, they are at their best young and fresh, when their dry delicacy makes them admirable accompaniments to the local freshwater fish and to the typical *fondues* and other cheese dishes of the region.

I have observed that Savoy's red wines are neither numerous nor noteworthy: none has been granted AOC rank save in a general sense, hyphenated with the regional name, but there are some among the VDQS wines, all or almost all from the hillsides just to the south and east of Chambéry, that Morton Shand found interesting enough, and capable, he wrote, of improving for as much as ten years or so in bottle. Some are made from the Gamay grape of Beaujolais, others from a local variety, the Mondeuse, of which I know nothing.

But whatever Lucien Tendret wrote in the eighteenth century, and Morton Shand in the twentieth, I should drink the red wines of Savoy as one drinks the whites – young: I doubt, indeed, whether today's growers can afford to tie up money in them while they age – no old Arbin, Montmelian or St-Jean-de-la-Porte has ever come my way, either in my native country or in its own.

The two individual AOC wines of Savoy are Crépy and Seyssel. Crépy comes from the hills north-east of Geneva, on the French side of the lake – a light, fresh white wine with a yellowish glint to it, made from Fendant or Chasselas grapes, as are the Swiss wines from the other side of Lake Geneva.

Seyssel is a little town on the Rhône, on the other side of Geneva. Its wines are usually made sparkling, and by the *méthode champenoise*: Hugh Johnson says of the sparkling Seyssel that it 'could be confused with champagne if anything could . . . dry, delicate and pale, it has the apéritif qualities to a high degree'. It is better-known in the United Kingdom now than when he wrote, in his book, *Wine*, that it is not often seen – many British shippers now import the sparkling Seyssel of the house of Varichon and Clerc, and it is the 'Club Special' sparkling wine of the London house of Justerini and Brooks.

It must have improved enormously, too, since Morton Shand wrote of it, in the 1960 edition of his book, that it was 'as fizzily characterless as still Seyssel is individual and excellent'. I get the impression that the consequent popularity abroad of the now much more carefully-made sparkling Seyssel, and its greater profitability (though it is much cheaper

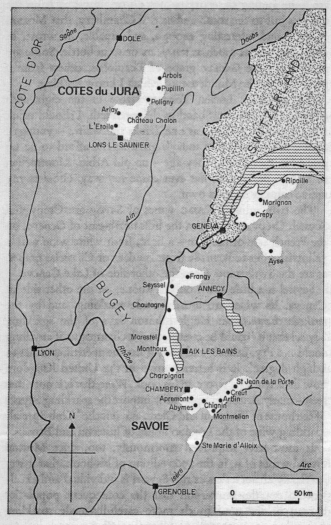

Map 5. The Jura and Savoy

than champagne) has led to more and more being produced, with a corresponding decline – as in Champagne – in the production of still wine. Why be satisfied with the profit on a bottle of still wine when the very same wine's tendency to sparkle in the spring following the vintage can be encouraged, and a bigger profit made?

But there is some still Seyssel to be found, and very light and clean it is.

So, too, the wine that is left with its natural *pétillance*, not given the full *méthode champenoise* sparkle, that is, but with the typical 'prickle' of a cool-climate or mountain-region wine held in by a wired-on cork. This is sold as Pétillant de Savoie, and I find it particularly refreshing as a summertime apéritif.

A great speciality of Savoy is the vermouth of Chambéry – lighter in flavour and drier than the better-known French vermouths of Marseilles, and the only vermouth entitled to its own *appellation*, an honour granted in 1932. Vermouth can be red or white, sweet or dry, lightly fortified with spirit, and flavoured with herbs and aromatics. That of Chambéry is dry, white and flavoured with local Alpine herbs.

At one time, Chambéry was known to hardly anyone in Britain save customers of the old Escargot Bienvenue restaurant in Soho, where it was a speciality of the house, and always offered to patrons as they studied the purple-ink, jellygraphed menu. (The custom still obtains, as does much of the old atmosphere of the Escargot, in spite of its having been taken over by a restaurant-chain.)

It was not taken up in any big way in Britain, in spite of the popularity of vermouths generally, and the ubiquity of the Martini cocktail, gin-and-It, gin-and-French, and gin-and-mixed, until a director of Gilbeys (now part of the IDV group), travelling in the United States in the nineteen-fifties, discovered his hosts in San Francisco making their martinis with it because it gave flavour and fragrance without loss of dryness and without, therefore, the need to overdo the gin. He arranged for his firm to take over the British agency for the Chambéry made by Dolin. Other Chambéry houses are Richard and Gaudin. Dolin make a delicious vermouth flavoured with wild strawberries, which is no longer imported into Britain, perhaps because it did not always maintain its freshness if kept hanging about in transit, or on a wine-merchant's shelf. It is worth seeking out on its home ground.

Finally, Savoy is the home of what most people regard as the greatest of strong, sweet after-dinner cordials – Chartreuse, green and yellow, made again at Grenoble by the Carthusian monks who had been expelled from France in 1903 but permitted to return in 1932.

This is a book about wine, not about liqueurs, but I cannot deny myself a respectful salute, if only in passing, to this noble compound, and the opportunity of repeating the story told me by the late and much-lamented Vyvyan Holland of how his father, Oscar Wilde, visiting the Grande Chartreuse monastery, asked the almoner the secret of the monks' patently serene happiness. 'One-third green, two-thirds yellow', said the almoner.

*

The *vignoble* of the Jura is tiny as wine-growing regions go, but it makes up in variety what it lacks in output, and two of its wines are unlike those of any other region.

The *vin jaune* of the Jura is made from the Savignan grape, which is not to be confused with the noble Sauvignon of Bordeaux and may be related either to the Tokay of Hungary or to the Palomino from which sherry is made.

However this may be, *vin jaune*, matured for a minimum of six years in wood, develops a crust of yeast, similar to the *flor* that covers the surface of *fino* sherry in cask. It is a strong, dry, nutty apéritif wine, not unlike an unfortified sherry or dry madeira, seldom met in Britain because its high alcoholic strength puts it into the fortified-wine range of duty and makes it as expensive as sherry or port. I find this a matter of indifference: I do not like the wine.

All parts of the small wine-growing area of the Jura make *vin jaune*, but the one with its own *appellation* is the district around Château-Chalon (a village, be it noted, not a château, though not big enough to appear in the Guide Michelin) and three adjoining villages.

All parts of the area also produce, but in very small quantities, a sweet, unfortified, dessert wine known as *vin de paille* because the grapes used to be spread out on straw mats (more usually now they are hung on wires) for two or three months to become almost raisin-like in the sun before being pressed.

The wine is matured for six to ten years in cask and is said to resemble, at its best, Imperial Tokay or a fine sweet madeira. I fancy that it is gradually going out of production because of the expense of the long, laborious process, and perhaps for lack of demand.

The other wines of the Jura are red, rosé and white, still and sparkling (*vin fou*) – most of them produced and marketed by the Arbois firm of Henri Maire, which dominates the wine trade of the region as no other region is dominated by one firm. That its vigorous marketing methods have done much to make the more common still and sparkling wines of the region well-known in other parts of France and abroad is indisputable. The effect of monopoly on quality is more debatable.

The white and the red Jura wines, even those with *appellations*, seem to be of only moderate quality outside their own district: drunk in the excellent restaurants of the little mountain towns, with the game, cheeses and particularly fine pork dishes of the region, they are delicious.

The pink wines, though – called *gris*, not *rosé* in these parts –

are another matter. I have never been much of a one for pink wine, that wine of compromise (save for pink champagne, which I dote upon), but the pink (or the grey) wines of the Jura in general, and more particularly those entitled to the Arbois *appellation*, are rivalled only by those of Tavel for fullness of flavour (some are almost more like light red wines than deep pink) and are perhaps clearer in colour and prettier in bouquet.

Arbois, the capital of Jura wines, an attractive country town in its own right, was the birthplace of Louis Pasteur, who conducted in his own vineyard and his own house there the experiments that resulted in the isolation of the microorganisms that bring about the fermentation of grape-juice.

Those of us who, for our writings about wine, have been decorated by the French Government with the Ordre du Mérite Agricole take pride in the fact that Pasteur was the first recipient of the decoration when it was instituted, in 1885.

THE WINES OF THE JURA AND SAVOY

AOC

Arbois

The *appellation* can apply to red, white and pink wines. The best reds are marketed under brand names (notably that of Frédéric Barberousse) by the almost monopolistic Jura firm of Henri Maire. The whites are dry, but full of flavour and fragrance, and the pink (or *gris*) wines are next, in my mind, only to Tavel for force of character.

Arbois-Pupillin

From a rather more restricted area just south of Arbois itself: I do not detect any difference in style or quality.

Arbois-Mousseux

Some sparkling wine is made in the region by the *méthode champenoise*, and only these – white and rosé – are entitled to this *appellation*.

The '*vin fou*' of the region is made by bottling at the peak of first fermentation and is not entitled to the *appellation*.

Château-Chalon

One of four villages that make the apéritif-like *vin jaune*, discussed earlier in this chapter.

Crépy

One of the few Savoy wines in the AOC list of this chapter. It is discussed in the introductory text (page 107).

Côtes de Jura

A comprehensive regional *appellation* for the red, white and rosé wines of the Jura. The regulations are strict, and the wines sound, but it can be assumed that wines with the more precise *appellation*, such as Arbois and L'Etoile, are probably rather finer.

Côtes de Jura Mousseux

As suggested above, probably not quite so fine as the sparkling Arbois and L'Etoile.

L'Etoile

The name of a district near the great cheese-producing town of Lons-le-Saunier (home of Comté, the French Gruyère). Mostly still and sparkling white wines, governed by the same rules as govern the *appellation* Arbois.

L'Etoile Mousseux

See above.

Roussette de Savoie

A white wine made specifically from what Morton Shand described as 'one of the best and most widely grown vines in Savoy'. Fresh and crisp, to be drunk young.

Seyssel
Seyssel Moussex

From Savoy: see introductory text of this chapter (p. 107).

Vin de Savoie

Red, white and rosé wines may qualify, but the only sparkling wine of the region must qualify specifically as Seyssel.

There are more whites than reds, and they are the better.

Fifteen districts may each add their names to 'Vin de Savoie': of these, the best (after Crépy and Seyssel, which have *appellations* of their own) are Apremont, Chautagne and Marignan for whites; Arbin, Montmelian and St-Jean-de-la-Porte for reds and rosés.

Vin de Savoie Mousseux

Similar in style, but not quite up to the quality of the sparkling Seyssel.

VDQS

All the wines under this heading are from Savoy, none from the Jura, and all from the hilly region 'woven in geometric patterns of vineyards', as Samuel Chamberlain put it,[*] known as Le Bugey, in the *départment* of the Ain, between Burgundy and the foothills of the Alps.

All are similar to, if not perhaps quite so distinguished as, the Savoy AOC wines listed above, except that they include

---

[*] S. Chamberlain, *Bouquet de France* (Hamish Hamilton, 1966).

pétillant wines – wines, that is, with a light sparkle, but not fully *mousseux*. They are particularly refreshing.

It would be otiose to append a note to each name: the characteristics will be clear from the notes on their AOC cousins, and from the introductory part of this chapter. Those VDQS denominations that are followed by a place-name are slightly stronger in alcohol than those without:

Mousseux du Bugey or Vin du Bugey Mousseux
Pétillant du Bugey or Vin du Bugey Pétillant
Roussette du Bugey
Roussette du Bugey followed by the name:

        Anglefort
        Arbignieu
        Chanay
        Lagnieu
        Montagnieu
        Virieu-le-Grand

Vin du Bugey
Vin du Bugey followed by the name:

        Cerdon
        Machuraz
        Manicle
        Montagnieu
        Virieu-le-Grand

Vin du Bugey Cerdon Pétillant
Vin du Bugey Cerdon Mousseux

For Further Reading

JEFFS, JULIAN, *The Wines of Europe*, Faber, 1971.
ROWE, VIVIAN, *French Wines, Ordinary and Extraordinary*, Harrap, 1972.

CHAPTER 6

The Rhône

THIS is where the south begins.

The wines of Burgundy, from the vineyards that run northwards from Lyons, although soft and full-bodied, are nevertheless cool-climate wines. As we have seen, *chaptalisation* is often necessary to give them enough alcohol for staying-power, and their generosity is balanced by sufficient acidity to give delicacy.

The wines of Bordeaux are grown between precisely the same latitudes as those of the Côte Rôtie and Hermitage, but the climate of the Bordelais is Atlantic, not Mediterranean.

What gives the wines of the Rhône their general family character, differ though they do from each other, is that from Lyons to the Mediterranean the Rhône valley is in summer perhaps as hot a region as any in France – hotter even than the Riviera, for there is no true sea-breeze, only the stuffy *mistral*, funnelled up between the slopes on either side of the river.

There are exceptions, of course – chiefly such wines as are grown in particularly light, sandy soil, or high up enough in the hills to enjoy a cooler micro-climate than their neighbours – but generally speaking the red wines of the Côtes du Rhône are fuller-bodied, fruitier in flavour, and of higher alcoholic strength than those of Burgundy and Bordeaux, the relatively few whites coarser or, at any rate, heavier in style, and the best rosé of the region one of the world's few really serious pink wines, because of its body and character.

The Côtes du Rhône vineyards lie on both sides of the river from immediately south of Lyons to just beyond Avignon, but not continuously. There are four main areas: these are, from

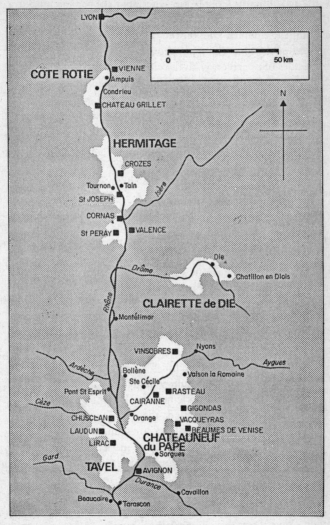

Map 6. The Rhône

north to south, the Côte Rôtie – literally, 'the roasted hillside'; the Hermitage region; an outlying area rather to the east, around the town of Die, on the river Drôme; and, by far the biggest of the four, the wine-growing area that stretches over both sides of the river, with the cities of Orange and Avignon in its middle, and the wines of Châteauneuf-du-Pape as its glory.

Taking each of these four areas in turn, and beginning at the north, the vineyards of the Côte Rôtie lie across the river from that gastronomic Mecca, the little country town of Vienne, with its famous three-star restaurant, the Pyramide, and other, less grand and less expensive, but no less serious establishments.

The Côte-Rôtie wines are the lightest and most elegant of the Rhône reds – partly because they come from the region's most northerly vineyards, partly because the best of these vineyards are between five and six hundred feet above sea-level, partly because about 5 per cent (in a few cases as much as 10 per cent) of juice from the white Viognier grape is combined with that of the black Syrah (or Sérine) in their making.

All the same, Côte Rôtie is a big wine by Bordeaux or Burgundy standards – Shand wrote of it that 'it has a glorious crimson colour, ample body, a fine bouquet, great suavity, and an incomparable satiny finish' – and it is usually rather higher in alcohol than burgundy or claret.

To the best of my knowledge, the Viognier is peculiar to this tiny district: from it is made the white wine of Condrieu, dry but full, and with a hint of sweetness and a flowery smell – a good wine to go with fish or fowl in rich, creamy sauces, and to be thus enjoyed, no doubt, at the two-starred Beau Rivage in the village of Condrieu itself, or Vienne's three-starred Pyramide, already mentioned.

Little comes to the United Kingdom – little, indeed, is made – save through such specialist shippers of Rhône (and, in his case, too, of Loire) wines as Robin Yapp of Mere, whose list is an enthusiast's guide to the wines of these two rivers.

The classic Condrieu is Château-Grillet, from the smallest vineyard – a mere three acres, producing only a thousand bottles or so a year – to be given an *appellation contrôlée* of its own. Spicy and scented, a deep gold in colour, it can be compared with a fine hock – certainly in price, and to some extent in style, though it has more backbone.

Farther downstream, twelve miles short of Valence, the great rock of Hermitage heaves itself above the Rhône like a riverside Gibraltar, giving its name to a wine that for long was at least as well-known in Britain as claret. Until a century ago, indeed, claret was often *hermitagé*: Warner Allen recorded in his *A History of Wine* that he was told by a most eminent burgundy-shipper that in his (the shipper's) grandfather's time 'practically the whole yield of Hermitage and Châteauneuf-du-Pape was destined to give colour, alcohol and body to feebler wines grown elsewhere, Hermitage being earmarked for Bordeaux, Châteauneuf for Burgundy'.

There is plenty of evidence from other sources that the practice was general and open – there was no deception about it. All I doubt in what the shipper said is the phrase 'practically the whole yield', for plenty of Hermitage was sold in this country under its own name and for its own sake.

Those great grand-tourists, Lords Bristol and Townshend, are known to have bought it at the very beginning of the eighteenth century; Fielding mentions it in his novels and Smollett in his *Travels*; Dr Middleton, in Sir Willoughby Patterne's cellar, chirrupped – yes, the word is Meredith's – that Hermitage 'has the light of the antique; the merit that it can grow to an extreme old age'; and, half-way between Meredith's time and ours, Saintsbury was calling it 'the manliest of wines'.

Then it went out of favour, perhaps because claret was so

cheap; now that clarets and burgundies have shot up in price, Hermitage is coming into its own again, though we usually drink it too young to know it at its best: we should mind Dr Middleton's words, and give it the chance to show the full-ness and depth of flavour that it develops with bottle-age.

The vineyards of Crozes-Hermitage are – I quote the Yapp list – peripheral to those of Hermitage; easier to work, be-cause flatter; less sandy, with more clay; and less well-exposed to the sun. So 'the wines exhibit precisely the same character-istics as Hermitage, but to a less marked degree'. They, too, improve enormously with bottle-age.

'Fat with a richness which fills your mouth, but also with a flinty edge', is Hugh Johnson's phrase for the white wine of this area, but I gather that some growers are giving their whites less time in wood than is traditional in the region, aim-ing at something like the freshness of the Loire wines. I doubt, though, if they will ever be so delicate.

At the southern end of this area, on the opposite side of the river from Valence, a full-flavoured sparkling white wine is made by the *méthode champenoise*, with the *appellation* Saint Péray (there is a still wine, too); and a lighter, faintly sweeter, fizz, Clairette de Die, comes from the outlying area on the Drôme, to the south-east.

South again, beyond the nougat town of Montélimar, and we are in the region of what a friend of mine used to amuse himself by calling 'Pope's Newcastle wine', which comes from around the village where Pope John XII, having built his Palace of the Popes at Avignon, built a new castle, eight miles to the north, as a summer residence.

Châteauneuf-du-Pape is the southernmost French wine of real distinction, the only Provençal wine that can claim to be a classic. Stronger in alcohol than burgundy or claret, and never anything like so elegant, it has as its best a magnificent bouquet.

A local puffing pamphlet says of it: 'it gives off a thousand

odours, violent at first, of truffles and of moorland herbs, and
then finer ones, the evocation of sun-kissed fruits, peaches and
apricots, an assortment of floral scents by the tubfull'. But
Keats did it better:

> 'Tasting of Flora and the country-green
> Dance, and Provençal song, and sunburnt mirth!'

This is the birthplace, too, of the laws of *appellation*, for in
the nineteen-twenties the local growers, inspired by one of the
greatest of French viticulturists, Baron le Roy de Boiseau-
marié, who was honoured by a statue in his lifetime, and who
until his death was president of the INAO, his creation, banded
themselves together to protect the name of their wines.

Similar to Châteauneuf, and promoted in 1971 to the same
AOC status are the wines of Gigondas, to the north-east of the
same region, and many of the reds of the region that are now
entitled to add their local name to the *appellation* Côtes du
Rhône: that of Vacqueyras is sometimes to be found in
British shops and restaurants.

On the other side of the river from Châteauneuf and
Avignon is Tavel, whence comes France's most distinguished
rosé – most distinguished, and yet disagreed about: Morton
Shand found it, 'beautifully clean to the palate, in colour a joy
to the eye, dry and yet *fruité* . . . just the right degree of flavour
and vinosity' whereas Edward Hyams called it 'quarrelsome',*
which can, of course, be said of any wine drunk perhaps too
eagerly, under a hot sun, and in the wrong company.

The point is that unlike so many rosés, Tavel is far from
being characterless and mawkish, but strong both in alcohol
and flavour: it grows in the wrong place for it to be taken as a
picnic wine. But its strength makes it both travel well and
keep well, and it is splendid for indoor buffet luncheons in
our misty island.

* Edward Hyams, *Vin* (Newnes, 1959).

Another outstanding wine comes from the other side of Châteauneuf – Beaumes de Venise, made from the Muscat grape, naturally sweet* but not at all heavily luscious, prettily fragrant, and drunk by the locals as an apéritif, though to English tastes it is a dessert wine that goes deliciously with fruit.

THE WINES OF THE RHÔNE

AOC

Château-Grillet

A great, full white wine from the Condrieu district in the northern group of Rhône-valley vineyards. See introductory section of this chapter (page 119).

Châteauneuf-du-Pape

The greatest red wine of the south, though Morton Shand idiosyncratically considered it 'less complex than Hermitage, and rather inferior to it in bouquet as in wealth and depth of flavour'. Hermitage is underrated, but this is to underrate the best Châteauneuf. See introductory paragraphs of this chapter (page 120). A certain amount of white Châteauneuf is made: it is dry and full-bodied, rather coarse compared with Loire whites and the best white burgundies.

Châtillon-en-Diois

Red, white and rosé – the red the lowest in alcohol, from the Hermitage district, or nearby, all sold through a cooperative in Die.

Clairette de Die

White and pale pink still wines from the hills to the east of

*Though permitted a limited degree of fortification (see Chapter 12).

the river valley. Most of the grapes here, though, are made into sparkling wine (see below).

Clairette de Die Mousseux
Sparkling wine, *méthode champenoise*, usually a little on the sweet side and with a hint of Muscat on the nose (both Clairette and Muscat grapes are used). Very pretty wine, but without the distinction of the other sparkler of the region, St-Péray (q.v.).

Condrieu
A very worthy white wine, of which Château-Grillet (q.v.) is the prime example, from the great restaurant country around Condrieu and Vienne. See introductory paragraphs (page 118).

Cornas
Pretty good, stout red wine from near Valence, just south of Hermitage – a sort of poor man's Hermitage or Châteauneuf that can go down very well, as Hugh Johnson points out, in the better restaurants of the region.

Coteaux du Tricastin
Red wines, rather light in strength and in body for this region, from between Orange and Montélimar. Not to be taken too seriously, but good picnic stuff.

Côtes du Rhône
A general *appellation* for the red, white and rosé wines of the region. If hyphenated with the names of any of the following fourteen *communes* (all in the southern stretch of the valley) then the quality is higher:

Cairanne	Saint-Maurice-sur-Eygues
Chusclan	Saint-Pantaléon-des-Vignes
Laudun	Séguret
Rasteau	Vacqueyras
Roaix	Valréas
Rochegude	Vinsobres
Rousset-les-Vignes	Visan

Côtes du Rhône-Villages
Also a cut above the simple Côtes du Rhône.

Côte Rotie
Overshadowed in popular esteem by those of the southern end of the valley, Châteauneuf and Hermitage, this – from the north – is held by some to be 'one of the best, if not the very best' (according to Hugh Johnson) of all the Rhône red wines. 'An almost claret-like delicacy and an irresistible raspberry-like scent', Mr Johnson goes on. I can taste the claret-like delicacy but cannot smell the raspberries.

Côtes du Ventoux
Red, white and rosé, from the southern end of the valley, towards Orange. The reds are the best, but rather thin, compared with the better Côtes du Rhône wines.

Crozes-Hermitage
Sort of cadet Hermitage – see below, and also the introductory paragraphs (page 120).

Gigondas
Another very distinguished red wine, from high country to the east of Orange. Morton Shand dismissed it briefly as the best of a rather ordinary lot, but a really good Gigondas falls not far short of a medium Hermitage or Châteauneuf – and that is higher praise than it may appear at first sight.

Hermitage
One of the great red wines of France: see introductory paragraphs (page 119).

Lirac
Not quite in the same class, but similar in style: from the same area that produces the Tavel rosé.

Saint-Joseph
One of the wines of the Cornas region (q.v.) near Valence, and a bit above its very good average.

Saint-Péray
Saint-Péray Mousseux
Some still, but more sparkling, white wine is made just south of the Cornas red-wine district. The still is light in alcohol but fullish in taste; the sparkling is a big wine, made by *méthode champenoise*, but fuller in flavour and deeper in colour.

They claim in these parts to have been making sparkling wines as long as the *champenois*: Arthur Hugh Clough, writing in the 1850s, sang,

> Your Chablis is acid, away with the Hock,
> Give me the pure juice of the purple Médoc:
> St Peray is exquisite; but, if you please,
> Some Burgundy just before tasting the cheese.
> So pleasant it is to have money, heigh-ho!
> So pleasant it is to have money.

Pleasant, too, to realize that in Britain sparkling Saint-Péray is about half the price of champagne.

Tavel
Probably the best pink wine of France: see introductory paragraphs (page 121).

VDQS

The VDQS wines of the Rhône need not detain us long, for the growers of the valley have succeeded in having all the wines of any quality promoted to AOC rank.

The following are sound, inexpensive, local-restaurant wines:

Coteaux de Pierrevert
Côtes du Luberon
Côtes du Vivarais
Côtes du Vivarais followed by the name:
    Orgnac
    Saint-Montant
    Saint-Remèze

These all come from the southern stretches of the Rhône valley, and resemble their Provençal neighbours.

Haut-Comtat
Red and rosé wines, full-flavoured and rather heady, from south of the Hermitage district.

For Further Reading

JEFFS, JULIAN, *The Wines of Europe*, Faber, 1971.

ROWE, VIVIAN, *French Wines, Ordinary and Extraordinary*, Harrap, 1972.

YAPP BROTHERS of Mere, Wiltshire, *Current* [Twice-yearly] *Price-Lists* (by application).

CHAPTER 7

Provence and Corsica

STRICTLY speaking, the townships of Châteauneuf-du-Pape and Tavel, which we came across in the previous chapter, are both in Provence, but their wines are Rhône wines: it is to their south and east that what are considered to be the Provençal vineyards stretch from Marseilles and Aix-en-Provence to Nice.

Their wines have never been highly regarded: Morton Shand devoted half a page to them in a book of more than three hundred, picking out fewer than a dozen wines by name of which 'the kindest thing that can be said is that they are the best of a poor enough lot'.

It is easy – all too easy – in the hot, dry south to grow high-yielding vines that produce common wine. And it is easy for the restaurants and cafés of the Riviera to sell it to thirsty sun-seeking holiday-makers from the north, who are disappointed when they get home again to find that the white Cassis or the red Bandol does not caress the palate anything like so appealingly in Manchester as in Menton, in Copenhagen as in Cannes.

They are coming up in the world, though: the tendency throughout southern France is to make rather better wine and achieve higher status for it. But the wine-growers of Provence should not, and will not, try too hard. Their wines will never command abroad anything like the prestige of the classic wines of France, and on their home ground they are suitably simple accompaniments to the aromatic, oily dishes of the region – *ratatouille* and *bouillabaisse*, *bourride* with *aïoli*, young

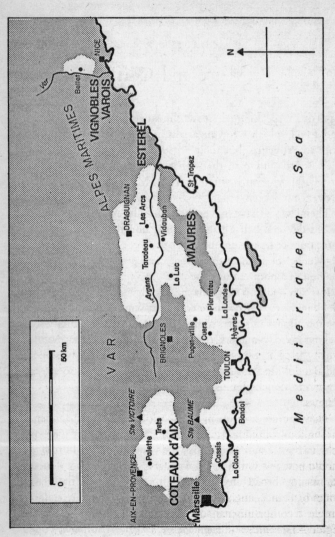

Map 7. Provence

lamb and even younger rabbit stuffed with herbs and in garlicky sauces – dishes that would overwhelm the subtler wines of cooler climes.

But Cassis (named after the picturesque little seaport near Marseilles, and not to be confused with *liqueur de cassis*, which is a blackcurrant cordial) goes well with the rich Marseillais fish dishes, the reds of Bandol with the even richer stews, and the pinks are suitably pretty for this coastline of bougainvillea and mimosa, orange-blossom and carnations, and of pretty girls wearing pretty little. As I have written elsewhere, the most suitable wine for summer-time picnic luncheons is 'wine of an engaging pink ... wine that looks pretty and need not be taken too damned seriously: a sort of popsy of a wine'. And this coast, pre-eminently, if not its hinterland – not by a long chalk – is popsy country.

*

The wines of Corsica, only very recently – in 1972 – elevated to A O C rank, are similar in some ways, yet different.

Like those of Provence they tend to be coarse, certainly to lack the finesse and delicacy of more northern wines, but they have much more character and body than the Provençal reds and whites – much more alcohol, too. 'Smiling Corsican brigands', Morton Shand called them, but admiringly, for he liked the scented island, and thought that its wines should be better-known.

Few are shipped to Britain that I know of, but *pieds noirs* from Algeria have been putting Corsican vineyards into good heart, and finding big markets in France for cheap wine, to be drunk under its own name or in blends.

In their own island, Corsican wines resemble some of the wines of Italy: indeed, they remind me particularly of the wines of the nearby island of Elba. As in Elba, and on the Italian mainland, a sweet red Aleatico is made, with a full

Muscat fragrance, and a sweet, Malaga-like *vin cotto*, or 'cooked' wine, made by reducing grape-juice over a fire to about half its original volume, adding as much uncooked must, and then fermenting and ageing. For those who like this sort of stuff, this is the sort of stuff they like.

THE WINES OF PROVENCE

AOC

Bandol or
Vin de Bandol

Red, white and rosé, from the slopes behind the busy little seaport and holiday-place of Bandol, a mere ten miles west of Toulon.

They have recently come up in the world: the reds, which are the best-known, are made chiefly from the Mourvèdre, which is said to have grown wild in these parts before the Romans came: they are usually pretty robust. The whites are similar to those of nearby Cassis (see below).

Bellet or
Vin de Bellet

Red, white and rosé, from the hills behind Nice and its holiday coast, in the cafés and restaurants of which most of it is drunk – it is on the list of half a dozen starred restaurants in Michelin. Pretty heady stuff, especially with a hot blue sky above and temptation of one sort or another round every corner.

Cassis

The *appellation* pertains to red, white and rosé, but it is the white that has the prestige – 'very dry, almost gritty', wrote Morton Shand, adding that it is 'much esteemed locally with

shellfish'. It is splendid with the flavoury fish stews of the
district (Marseilles, the capital of *bouillabaisse*, is only about
fifteen miles away).

Not to be confused with the blackcurrant cordial of the
same name (sometimes *crème de cassis*) from Dijon.

Palette

From the hills around Aix-en-Provence, and more highly
regarded than any of the other Provence wines, thanks largely
to the efforts of one particular estate, that of Château Simone.
Shand regarded the red, white and rosé as 'excellent table
wines', which is more than he said of any other wines of the
region: it is generally agreed that the red is the best – it has
an especially satisfying bouquet.

VDQS

Coteaux d'Aix-en-Provence
Coteaux de Baux-de-Provence
Côtes de Provence

Local wines from less strictly defined areas than those above,
but reaching certain specified standards of quality, by specified
methods, can qualify for VDQS status. The whites and rosés
should be drunk young and well-chilled; the reds are full-
bodied. Puget-Ville, Taradeau and Pierrefeu are good areas,
but not accorded individual status.

It is significant, though, that the starred restaurants of
Baux-de-Provence, including the resoundingly famous
Oustau de Baumanière, do not list their named local wine in
Michelin, but prefer wines from the Rhône.

THE WINES OF CORSICA

AOC

Vin de Corse
Vin de Corse Patrimonio
Vin de Corse Coteaux d'Ajaccio
Vin de Corse Sartène or Coteaux du Sartenais
Vin de Corse Calvi
Vin de Corse Figari
Vin de Corse Porto Vecchio

All the AOC wines of Corsica were given their accolade together – at the end of 1972.

It is virtually impossible to distinguish between them: they are all cheap enough for visitors to while away happy hours in comparative tastings.

Let them beware, though: they are headier than they seem, especially as most of them are white or pink, and easy to drink, well-chilled, at picnics in the *maquis*.

Not given individual status, but commended by Shand, are the white from around Bonifacio and the red Tallano, both in the south, and the reds, whites and rosés of Patrimonio, in the north.

For Further Reading

JEFFS, JULIAN, *The Wines of Europe*, Faber, 1971.

ROWE, VIVIAN, *French Wines, Ordinary and Extraordinary*, Harrap, 1972.

WOON, BASIL, *The Big Little Wines of France*, Wine & Spirit Trade Publications, 1972.

CHAPTER 8

Languedoc and Roussillon

THE French cling to the historic names of their regions long after they have ceased to have a precise geographical or administrative reality. A Frenchman knows himself to be a Norman or a Gascon or a Champenois, though there has been no Normandy or Gascony or Champagne for these past couple of centuries.

The Languedoc was originally the country of the *langue d'oc*, where the word for 'yes' was '*oc*', and not that of the *langue d'oil*, where it was '*oil*' (and has become '*oui*').

Very roughly, the Languedoc was originally the region, from the Mediterranean to the Loire, in which, before the legions withdrew, Gauls had made of the Latin of the Roman soldiers their own relaxed, Romance, language: to the north, Teutonic Franks took to demotic Latin as a foreign tongue, and spoke it more stiffly.

Eventually, the name became applied formally to a much more restricted region, consisting largely of the Mediterranean coast west of the Bouches du Rhône and its hinterland, along with an inland area northwards from Nîmes as far as St Etienne.

At the Revolution this was split into *départements*, and what the INAO now regards as the Languedoc lies in the *départements* of Aude, Hérault, and part of Gard.

Along with this region, for the INAO's purposes, goes the small historic region of Roussillon, more precisely defined geographically by its present official name of Pyrénées Orientales.

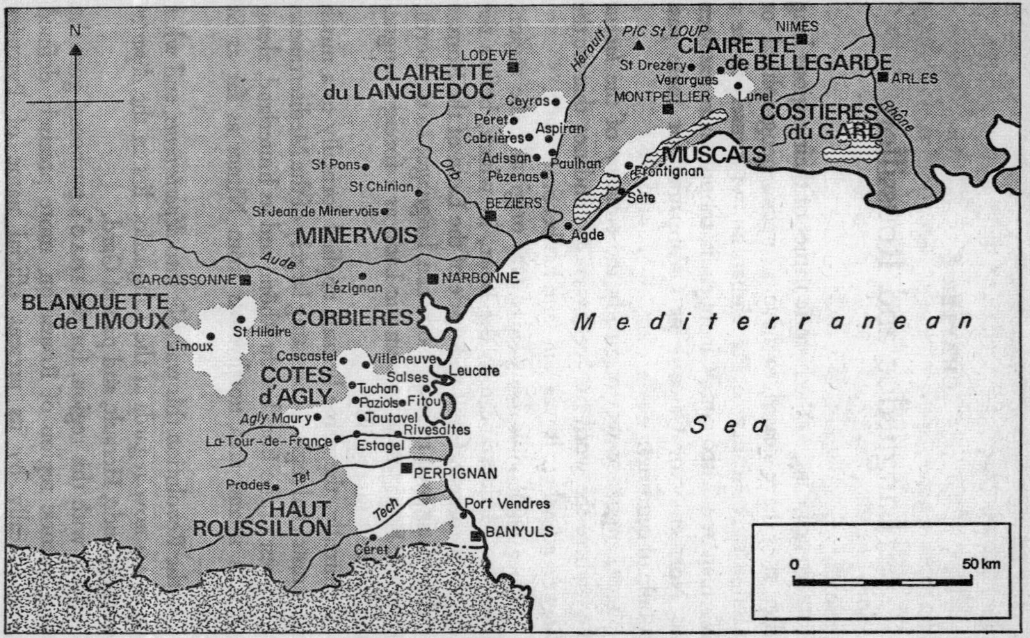

Map 8. Languedoc and Roussillon

The whole area is a sea of vines: this is the most productive wine-growing area of France – and the least distinguished.

This is where the *pinard* of the French soldier comes from, the working-man's pint (and more) – wine often so weak in character and low in alcohol that it has to be given guts by an admixture of wine from North Africa or, perhaps, these days, from Spain or Portugal or Italy.

The weakness of these wines of the south seems a contradiction of the general rule that sunnier climes produce heavier wines. But type of vine is a factor, too, which is why some are considered as 'noble', some not, and why for a wine to be given AOC or VDQS rank it has to be made only of certain specified grapes. In this region, poor but prolific vines produce poor, thin wine, where 'classic' vines such as the Pinot of Burgundy or the Cabernet of Bordeaux would yield strapping stuff.

When an Englishman sees, and is surprised by, a French peasant or private soldier swigging wine like tea, he should remind himself that the stuff probably comes from these parts and is not much stronger.

All the same, there are pockets of, as it were, resistance to this tide of mediocrity: small areas dotted throughout the region, from the foothills of the eastern Pyrenees to the western banks of the lower Rhône, where good – if never very remarkable – wines are made, thanks to a particular microclimate, to a vine of quality, and usually to a combination of one or both of these conditions with long local tradition.

Thus, Clairette de Bellegarde, from just south of Nîmes, a white wine with yellowish tinges, must be made exclusively from the Clairette grape, comply with the usual restrictions as to pruning and production per acre, and pass a tasting test to qualify for its *appellation* and, right at the other end of the region, is the red Collioure, given its *appellation* only in 1971.

Largely through the establishment of modern cooperatives,

the increased demand both in France and in such traditional markets as Britain for sound, consistent but cheaper alternatives to AOC wines is being met by an improvement in the product of the huge vineyard-covered stretches of Minervois and Corbières. These are now the biggest VDQS areas in the south of France, and their names are becoming familiar in British wine-merchants' lists: Justerini and Brooks, for instance, have been selling them since 1973, and at little more than £1 a bottle.

Before leaving this very picturesque region ('hot and handsomely savage' is Edmund Penning-Rowsell's phrase for it, in his *Red, White and Rosé*) we must mention its sweet wines – 95 per cent of France's *vins doux naturals* (VDN) and *vins de liqueur* (VDL) come from this corner of the country, some from around Frontignan, which is on the coast between Sète and Montpellier, but most from around Perpignan, and from there to the Spanish frontier.

The difference between VDL and VDN is not, as might be supposed, that between fortified and unfortified.* Both types are fortified with alcohol, the VDN (usually green label) with from 5 to 10 per cent, the VDL (usually orange label) with 15. They are made from Muscat grapes, are often – surprisingly – red or red-gold, as well as straw-coloured or rosé, and are drunk cool, whether as apéritifs or as dessert wines.

Not so delicate as the Beaumes de Venise mentioned in a previous chapter, these wines are nevertheless pleasant enough, with their intense flavour and fragrance of the Muscat grape.

Pleasant enough, that is, save when they take on with age the madeira-like smell and flavour referred to in these parts, and favourably, as *rancio*, more to the liking of the locals, I fancy, than of visitors.

---

*See Chapter 12, page 189.

THE WINES OF LANGUEDOC AND ROUSSILLON

AOC

Clairette de Bellegarde *or* Belgarde
White wine from a ridge overlooking the Camargue, south of Nîmes: see introductory text to this chapter (page 135).

Clairette de Languedoc
Similar style of wine, from the same grape, but from farther west, more plentiful, and headier.

Collioure
Full-bodied red Roussillon wine from the foothills of the eastern Pyrenees, on the Spanish frontier.

Fitou
Deep in colour, a strong but soft and velvety red wine from a circle of *communes* in the Fitou area, some along the coast, some on the hills behind, between Narbonne and Perpignan. Quite the best red wine of the region.

VDQS

Cabrières
A very dry rosé from the area of the Coteaux de Languedoc (q.v.).

Corbières
Corbières Supérieures
Red, white and rosé wines from the vast area of vineyards of the *département* of the Aude. Regulations the same for both, save that the *supérieures* have to reach a higher alcoholic content.

Costières du Gard

Red, white and rosé wines produced in large quantities in the hilly country between Nîmes and the coast. Some of the reds – full-bodied and strong – are imported into Britain, but none is outstanding. They are better where they are, with the flavoury Provençal food.

Coteaux du Languedoc

Reds, whites and rosés, moderate in strength as in quality, from such scattered *communes* strung out between Nîmes and Narbonne as make the modest grade. They are entitled to hyphenate their names to the generic title: some are permitted to leave out the generic 'Coteaux du Languedoc':

Cabrières	Pic-Saint-Loup
Coteaux de la Méjanelle	Quatourze
Coteaux de Saint-Christol	Saint-Chinian
Coteaux de Vérargues	Saint-Drézéry
Faugères	Saint-Georges-d'Orques
La Clape	Saint-Saturnin
Montpeyroux	

Côtes du Cabardès et de l'Orbiel *or* Cabardès

All I know is that this comes from north-west of Carcassonne: I cannot find the region on the map, and I do not know whether the wine is red or white.

Côtes du Roussillon
Côtes du Roussillon-Villages

Strong red, white and rosé wines from the Pyrenean foothills: the Villages wines are from the more favoured sites, stronger and capable, it is said, of improvement with age.

Minervois
Reds and whites (the whites are the stronger) from between Carcassonne and Narbonne.

Picpoul-de-Pinet
The Picpoul is the Piquepoule from which armagnac is still made and the Folle Blanche from which cognac used to be made until it was replaced there by the St Emilion.

Under the hot sun of the Hérault it makes a strong, hard white wine.

Roussillon-dels-Aspres
Lightish wines from upper slopes of the region: Vivian Rowe prefers the white, the rosé and the red in that order.

Vin Noble de Minervois or Minervois Noble
Well, 'noble' seems pitching it a bit strong, but it indicates Minervois wines (see above) of greater strength than the ordinary – 13 degrees as against the 10 and 11, respectively for the usual VDQS red and white. This is getting on for sherry strength, and heady for a table wine.

For Further Reading

JEFFS, JULIAN, *The Wives of Europe*, Faber, 1971.

ROWE, VIVIAN, *French Wines, Ordinary and Extraordinary*, Harrap, 1972.

WOON, BASIL, *The Big Little Wines of France*, Wine & Spirit Trade Publications, 1972.

CHAPTER 9

The South-West

THE region designated by INAO as the South-West has no geographical homogeneity – it stretches from the Dordogne in the north to the Basque country on the mountainous Spanish border, and as far as the rose-red city of Albi, a quarter, let us say, as old as time, on the banks of the Tarn.

The authorities even include among the wines listed under this heading the sparkling white wine, Blanquette de Limoux, which comes from near Carcassonne and which to my mind would be more appropriately regarded as one of the wines of Languedoc-Roussillon.

Here it is, though, along with other sparkling wines from Gaillac, between Albi and Montauban, sweet wines from Monbazillac, pink wines from the Pyrenees, strong reds from Irouléguy and that even stronger red, the 'black wine' of Cahors, on the Lot.

It can be seen that there is no more common character to the wines than homogeneity to the countryside. What makes them interesting, indeed, is the intense individuality of each, and it is easier to deal with them individually, in the list that follows, than to attempt to find a family likeness that does not exist.

THE WINES OF THE SOUTH-WEST

AOC

Béarn

Bergerac

The *appellation* is granted to both the red and the white wines – there are more whites than reds – provided the usual AOC

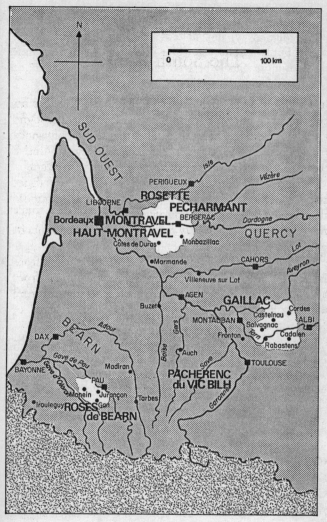

Map 9. The South-West

conditions are observed. The grape varieties are those of the Bordeaux region (the eastern extremity of which is only a dozen miles away) and the reds are not unlike minor clarets, lighter but less subtle, the whites sometimes sweet, sometimes dry, but more usually betwixt and between, like some of the less dry Graves, or Entre-Deux-Mers.

The town of Bergerac has an interesting and very go-ahead Maison du Vin, much more a place for tasting-rooms and laboratories than for museum pieces, and a Musée du Tabac for good measure – this is a great tobacco-growing region. The restaurant named after Rostand's Cyrano de Bergerac is starred in Michelin; its cuisine, like that of the whole of the glutton's pleasure-garden that is Périgord, bases itself on truffles, walnuts, geese, duck, and their livers, and truffles again.

Bergerac Sec
The driest of the local whites, rather like a dry Graves, and crisp enough to counterbalance the ponderously rich Périgourdine dishes.

Blanquette de Limoux
A *méthode champenoise* sparkler from the beautiful Aude valley, near Carcassonne.

It has a hint of sweetness, and less character than such other *méthode champenoise* wines as Seyssel or Saint-Péray, from the Rhône. Alexis Lichine says of it that it is an 'argument for drinking only real champagne'.

Cahors
Now here is an interesting wine, the so-called 'black wine' of Cahors, which was being shipped to England before claret was, and until given its *appellation* in 1971 the senior VDQS wine in France.

Made from the Malbec grape; intensely deep in colour; and with apparently infinite capacity for ageing, which does not necessarily mean that it grows in majesty like claret. Indeed, a friend speaks warmly of Cahors *de l'année*. Morton Shand thought it indifferent, but it is big, robust stuff, heartening when heartening is called for, and full in the nose, as in the mouth.

In the old days, this district shipped sweet red wines to northern and eastern Europe – the Russians still call one of their sweeter Crimean wines 'Kaoursky'.

Côtes de Bergerac
Red and white: see Bergerac, above.

Côtes de Bergerac Moelleux
Côtes de Bergerac-Côtes de Saussignac
The more luscious of the local white wines, which would be Monbazillac if they could. See below.

Côtes de Buzet
From near Agen, the plum town, and not far, therefore, from the south-easternmost tip of the Bordelais: these wines used to be marketed as Bordeaux. The reds are like fairly full clarets; the whites like very dry Graves; I think that the rosés of the district are not entitled to the *appellation*. Whites and reds are both better than one would assume from the fact that, although mentioned (as following the Bordeaux style) in Julian Jeff's *The Wines of Europe*, they do not appear in any of the other usual English works of reference: Shand, Simon, Lichine, Johnson, Vandyke Price. Many less interesting wines do.

Côtes de Duras
Red and white from the south-western edge of the Bergerac *appellation* region, and adjacent to the Bordelais. Morton

Shand noted their family resemblance to Bordeaux – but they are very much a cadet branch.

Côtes de Montravel

White. Also on the edge of the Bergerac region, and adjacent to the Bordelais. These wines have seemed to me to be lighter than the neighbouring whites, though they are – and are required by *appellation* to be – semi-sweet in style and with 12·5 degrees of alcohol, which is not far short of the 13 degrees required of Sauternes.

Fronton
Côtes du Fronton or Frontonnais

Along with Villaudric (see below), described by Shand as 'sometimes a rather disagreeable and dead sort of red wine'. From between Gaillac and Toulouse, in which latter city it seems to be highly regarded.

Gaillac
Gaillac Premières Côtes
Gaillac Doux
Gaillac Mousseux

The *appellation* entitlements of these wines date from before the war and, as Hugh Johnson observes in his *Atlas*, Gaillac is the biggest of the 'few areas of France which are *Appellation Contrôlée* but which hardly make the wine they must once have made to earn the title'.

'Gaillac', *tout court*, can be red, white or pink. It is most likely to be white; the reds are more like Rhône wines than clarets in style, without being all that stylish. The whites are more likely to be sweet than dry; the *appellation* 'Premières Côtes' is reserved for sweet; the other *appellations* speak for themselves.

Haut-Montravel

Virtually the same as Côtes de Montravel (q.v.), but from a rather more restricted area, very slightly less permitted yield, and similarly slightly less alcohol.

Irouléguy

When I first came across this wine – through a Welsh shipper, Jones-Pughe of Cardiff – I wrote in a newspaper article that 'it is full in flavour and in fragrance, more of a wine for dinner than for luncheon, and for autumn than for summer – it would go well with game'.

It is the only A O C Basque wine: it comes from a cooperative in the south-westernmost corner of France where most of the growers and cellarmen speak Basque, and its bitter finish derives from a local grape, the Tannat, softened by some of the minor Bordeaux breeds.

Jurançon

Who am I to be the first wine-writer not to tell the story of how, as soon as he was born, in Pau, the future Henri IV, the *vert galant*, had his lips touched with a clove of garlic and then moistened with a few drops of Jurançon from a golden goblet?

Catherine de Medici used to call Henri 'le Béarnais', and the grapes of which Jurançon is made – Gros and Petit Manseng and Courbu – are *tout à fait* Béarnais because, according to André Simon, they are grown nowhere else.

There is a dry Jurançon, but the classic is sweet, made in the same way as Sauternes, after the grapes have been rotted on the vine by the *pourriture noble*, but aged longer in wood. Simon found a truffle-like quality in the bouquet; others have written of peaches, carnations and cloves. It is clearly a wine of highly individual character, but it is not so easy to like as Monbazillac, say, or Sauternes.

Limoux Nature

A still white wine from the same region as Blanquette de Limoux (q.v.) and even less well-known.

Madiran

Sturdy, red wine from the banks of the Adour, between the Armagnac brandy country and the Pyrenees: notably heavy to the nose.

Monbazillac

Not even in its great years so unctuously rich as the great Sauternes, nor with the underlying subtleties of even the fullest of the German *trockenbeerenauslesen*, this is nevertheless one of Europe's best natural (which is to say unfortified) dessert wines. In poor years, the wine is merely sweetish, and light in texture.

It comes from the Bergerac district, where they drink it with the local *pâté de foie gras*, as do the Bordelais their Sauternes and Barsacs.

Montravel

See Côtes de Montravel and Haut-Montravel: if Monbazillac is the poor man's Sauternes this is the poorer man's Monbazillac.

Pacherenc-du-Vic-Bilh

This oddly-named white wine comes from the same area as the red Madiran: I have not only never tasted, but never even seen it, but I read that it has reddish-brown tinges, and am not surprised to be told that it is full-bodied and fruity.

Pécharmant

Lichine considers this to be the best of the Bergerac reds, and

I have certainly come across bottles that could have passed as St Emilions. Good with game and pretty rich stews.

Rosette
In spite of what one would expect from the name, this is white – from Bergerac and semi-sweet, which gives it the substance and fragrance to stand up to the truffled dishes of the region.

Vin de Blanquette
There is a subtle distinction between this and Blanquette de Limoux (q.v.). The Blanquette is *méthode champenoise*: the Vin de Blanquette goes through the secondary fermentation in bottle without *disgorgement*. It has never come my way, and I cannot pronounce on it.

VDQS

Côtes du Marmandais
Red and white wines from the Garonne valley between Bergerac and Buzet that make pleasant on-the-spot drinking.

Rosé de Bearn
Picnic stuff.

Tursan
No reference book I know of lists this wine: it can be red, white or pink; it comes from the Basque country. The red is not so good as the Irouléguy of the same region, and Shand thought that the best of the Tursans was the white – it is pretty heady stuff, though.

Vin d'Entraygues et du Fel
Vin d'Estaing
Vin de Lavilledieu
Vin de Marcillac

The '*vin de*' any named region, given VDQS status, is the local red, white or rosé, or all three, once it has attained a reasonable level of character and consistency. These of the south-west are all sound beverage wines, very enjoyable when drunk locally, with regional dishes, but seldom met with in Britain save, perhaps, under brand names.

Of these, the d'Estaing is perhaps the best red.

For Further Reading

JEFFS, JULIAN, *The Wines of Europe*, Faber, 1971.

ROWE, VIVIAN, *French Wines, Ordinary and Extraordinary*, Harrap, 1972.

WOON, BASIL, *The Big Little Wines of France*, Wine & Spirit Trade Publications, 1972.

CHAPTER 10

Bordeaux

THE richest and the proudest corner of the vast vineyard that is France is the Bordelais.

One square mile in every eight of the five thousand square miles of the *département* of the Gironde, of which the great city of Bordeaux is the centre and the capital, is under vines.

Each year, on an average, these five hundred square miles of vines produce something not far short of one-tenth of all the wines of France.

True, the Midi produces even more, but of nothing like the quality, whereas two-thirds of the Gironde's annual output is of AOC standard. No place in the world produces so much fine wine – between one-third and two-fifths of all French AOC wines, from the great luscious white dessert wines of the Sauternais, the pretty wooded country that stretches thirty miles or so up the river Garonne from Bordeaux, to the full red wines of Pomerol and of the postcard-picturesque little medieval city of St Emilion, on the other side of the Dordogne; and from the light, dry and semi-sweet white wines of Entre-Deux-Mers – the land between the rivers, which is to say the Dordogne and the Garonne, before they meet to form the Gironde – by way of the finer whites and reds of the Graves, around Bordeaux itself, to the reds of Bourg and Blaye on one side of that estuary and of the Médoc on the other.

Let us take first the white wines of Bordeaux.

Around the city of Bordeaux itself, and stretching south-eastwards from it along the left bank of the Garonne is the Graves, a district that takes its name from its gravelly soil.

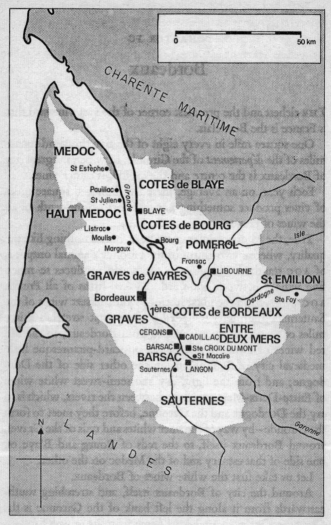

Map 10. Bordeaux

Both red and white wines are grown here, and we shall consider the reds later. The white Graves can be *demi-sec* or dry, but in even the driest Graves I find a hint of sweetness, as well as a sort of earthiness. The Bordelais drink dry white Graves (or the dry Entre-Deux-Mers) with the delicious oysters of nearby Arcachon, but I would prefer, myself, a crisper accompaniment from the Loire, say, or from Alsace.

Within the southern stretch of the Graves is the bosky enclave of the Sauternais, a region of modestly light sweet white wines, marketed simply as Sauternes (or Barsac) and also of great, lusciously rich dessert wines, sold under their château names, such as Yquem, Coutet, Climens and others.

The sweetness derives from the *pourriture noble*, or noble rot – *Botrytis cinerea* to the scientist, and not to be confused with the disastrously damaging ordinary rot, *pourriture grise*.

In a warm, damp autumn the white grapes turn pinkish and then begin to shrivel until they look like mouldy sultanas. The water-content of the juice evaporates, leaving a concentrate of sugar and flavour.

In minor vineyards, the growers pick all the grapes at once, as soon as any have been affected, unable to do as the swagger châteaux do, which is to go through their vineyards over and over again, picking *only* the individual grapes that have been attacked by the rot.

So ordinary Sauternes, entitled only to that simple *appellation* (or the *appellation* Barsac, as explained below) will be sweet but light, whereas at such a château as Yquem, as I learned when I visited it in 1974, a row of vines may well be picked ten or eleven times between the beginning of October, say, to as late as the middle of November (the vintage *has* ended as late as mid-December!) and produces a golden wine, almost oily in its richness, with a remarkably intense fragrance, flavour and sweetness.

Four communes other than Sauternes itself are permitted

that *appellation* (given – this must always be understood – that all the INAO regulations are observed). They are Bommes, Fargues, Preignac and Barsac: this last may use the *appellation* either Barsac or Sauternes.

In years when the weather of autumn does not encourage the onset of the noble rot, or when the Sauvignon grapes do much better than the Sémillon, they make a dry white wine at Yquem, named Ygrec. Some other châteaux, notably Filhot, make a dry as well as a sweet wine every year – the market for lusciously sweet white wine is limited.

Such wines are not entitled to the Sauternes *appellation*, reserved for the sweet of the region; they are 'Bordeaux Supérieur'.

The Sauternais can drink their richest and most unctuous wines with the *pâté de foie gras* of the Landes and with roast *pré salé* mutton from Pauillac: I cannot. A tiny glass after a meal – no more – is my ration, and I have already quoted in my introduction what Raymond Postgate designated as 'the right company'. And the dry wines seem to me unbalanced, as though Providence had meant them to be sweet, and their destiny had been wilfully rough-hewed.

Sweet white wines are grown across the river, around Loupiac and Ste-Croix-du-Mont, that are still harder to sell than the lesser Sauternes and Barsacs; in the wide spread of pretty, wooded country that lies between the Garonne and the Dordogne, and is consequently called Entre-Deux-Mers, they grow white wines of modest quality, dry to medium-sweetish.

So much for the white wines of the Bordelais. Red wine is grown on the edge of the Entre-Deux-Mers district, along the right bank of the Garonne, with the *appellation* Premières Côtes de Bordeaux: it is sound table wine, like the red wines of Bourg, Blaye and Fronsac but, like these, is overshadowed by the princely clarets of the Médoc, Pomerol, St Emilion and Graves.

Many of us – and I use the word 'us' deliberately – consider that from these four regions come the noblest red wines in the world. This, of course, is opinion, not fact, and if burgundy-lovers protest that the very greatest burgundies are nobler still, that also is opinion, whereas it is fact, that they themselves admit, that whichever are the greatest of all, there are *more* truly great clarets than there are truly great burgundies.

I have already written, in the chapter on burgundies, that there is more similarity than difference between the two wines and, indeed, that some clarets and some burgundies can easily be mistaken for each other. The clarets of Pomerol and St Emilion particularly are more like burgundies than those of the Médoc.

At their best, claret is more subtle than burgundy, with more layers, so to speak, of complex flavour and fragrance; burgundy more bland and more, perhaps, immediately winning, but with less depth.

At their worst, claret can be sharp and thin, burgundy flabby.

But, as I have suggested in a previous chapter, it is absurd to exaggerate their differences, or to suppose that a claret-lover cannot enjoy a good burgundy, or t'other way round.

*

For three hundred years – from the marriage in 1152 of Eleanor of Aquitaine to Henry of Anjou (soon to be Henry II of England) until the fall of Bordeaux in 1453 – the whole of the Bordelais was in obedience to successive kings of England.

It is only in the English-speaking countries that the red wine of Bordeaux is known generically as 'claret', as it has been since the fourteenth century, if not earlier, when a couple of hundred ships would leave Bordeaux for Bristol, London and other English ports laden with about 80 per cent of England's annual consumption of wine.

In those days, and until the seventeenth century or later, it was the wine grown nearest to Bordeaux that was best-known and best-liked. The Médoc was marshy, and communications were bad. It is significant that the first known mention in English literature to a named single-vineyard claret was a Graves, in Samuel Pepys's entry in his diary for 10 April 1663: '... to the Royall Oak Tavern in Lumbard Street ... and here drank a sort of French wine, called Ho Bryan, that hath a good and most particular taste that I never met with'.

In the course of the next century the Médoc was drained and developed, and took a lead in the production of fine red wines that it has never lost.

Less than another century later, when Prince Napoleon, the Emperor's cousin, called for a classification of the red wines of the *département* of the Gironde for the Paris Exhibition of 1855, all sixty-two of the wines selected to be named and classified – to become *crus classés* – were from the Médoc, with only one exception: Pepys's Haut Brion, a red Graves.

The list is given at the end of this chapter – it stands now exactly as it did in 1855 with one exception: by a decree of the French Government in 1973, the *premier crus* were reclassified, and Château Mouton-Rothschild took its rightful place among them.

Classifications of clarets, based on the prices they commanded, had been in existence for a century before 1855: this was the first to be commissioned by a governmentally appointed body and officially drawn up. It was realized at the time that it was the most important ever made, and the committee went to great pains to give it as permanent a validity as they could, and took into account not only the prices prevailing at the time, but those of many years past, and also the soil and the subsoil of each vineyard.

The list is still a good, though by no means a perfect, guide to the relative quality of these sixty-two wines. But that is all, and it must not be allowed to mislead.

In the *département* of the Gironde there must be now, and may well have been then, a couple of thousand named, single-vineyard wines.

What the classification of 1855 did was to select from these a mere sixty-two peers of the realm, as it were – and I use the analogy deliberately, for there are five ranks of the *crus classés*, precisely as there are of the British peerage: Lafite and the other first growths are dukes; Léoville-Barton, for example, a marquess; Palmer an earl; Beychevelle a viscount; Cantemerle a baron.

So every claret listed in the 1855 classification is a nobleman – one of a mere sixty-two to be picked from a couple of thousand to appear in the Debrett of clarets.

This is more to the point than to think of a fifth growth as being in some sense *fifth-rate* compared to a first. And just as in Britain any peer other than a duke is addressed simply as 'Lord' so-and-so, whether he is the latest in a long line of marquesses or a newly created life baron, so each of the classified clarets other than a first growth refers to itself on its label not as a second or third but as a *grand cru classé* – a lord.

After the classed growths come the *crus exceptionnels* (an unofficial but widely recognized category), then the formally accepted *crus bourgeois* and *crus artisans*, as we might refer to baronets, knights and esquires, but it must be made clear that these are not *appellations*: single châteaux do not have individual *appellations* of their own.

Lafite, for instance, would be entitled to style itself 'Bordeaux, *appellation contrôlée*' but, rather better, it is 'Médoc'. Finer again, because more restricted, and with higher standards still, it is 'Haut Médoc', and within the *appellation* 'Haut Médoc' is the most restricted of these, as it were, concentric circles, the *appellation* granted to the *com-*

mune, Pauillac, within which Lafite lies, and the name of which it bears on its label.

Beyond that, a château can apply only its own standards: a wine could fail to come up to the standard that Lafite sets for itself, and still be entitled to the *appellation* 'Pauillac', and there are years when a château as proud as Lafite does *déclasser* some of its wine and sell it under the *commune appellation* only.

Comparisons between the various *communes* of the Médoc and between the Médoc and the other red wine-growing regions of the Bordelais will be found in the list of *appellations*. It must be mentioned here, though, that although there is a family resemblance between all clarets, there are differences between one another that may depend upon soil, subsoil, micro-climate, or the varying proportions of the permitted grapes that are grown at this château or at that.

In the Médoc the most important of the varieties permitted by INAO are the Cabernet Sauvignon and the Merlot. Here, the Cabernet Sauvignon gives depth and colour to a wine, as well as the tannin from pips and skin that provides backbone and staying power; the Merlot is more difficult to rear but gives softness, fragrance and fruitiness.

Thus, neighbouring vineyards will produce wines noticeably different from each other according to the proportions of each: Lafite is lighter and more delicate than Mouton, Mouton sturdier and 'bigger' than Lafite, because Lafite comprises about five times as much Merlot as at Mouton, and only two-thirds as much of the Cabernet Sauvignon.

The choices, of course, are deliberate: each château has its house-style, which it is proud of, and eager to maintain.

Upstream, and on the other side of the river from Bordeaux, are the twin districts of St Emilion and Pomerol.

The soil is richer here than in the Médoc, and more Merlot is grown, as well as Malbec, which is grown in the Médoc only in very small proportions and which, like the Merlot, produces a softer, fruitier wine than the Médoc's predominant Cabernet-Sauvignon.

The wines of St Emilion were officially classified in 1955 – a whole century after what was officially a classification of the whole *département* of the Gironde, but which turned out to be only of the Médoc (plus Haut-Brion from the Graves) because in 1855 no St Emilion or Pomerol was reckoned to be in the same class, because none had been fetching the same price, as any of the top sixty-odd from the Médoc.

Nowadays, Cheval Blanc and Ausone, of the St Emilions and, pre-eminently, Petrus, a Pomerol, are as highly regarded – and as highly priced – as any of the Médoc first growths.

It is among the lesser growths of these two neighbouring regions that the amateur of good claret will make some of his happiest finds.

Softer and fruitier than the more reserved Médocs, they wear their hearts on their sleeves, so to speak and, being quicker to mature, they are cheaper – money has been tied up in them for a shorter time before they are on sale as ready to drink.

It is pleasant to take an apéritif of dry white Graves in Libourne, the busy little market town that is the centre of the St Emilion and Pomerol trade, and then drive on the couple of miles to the picturesque but not unduly self-conscious walled town of St Emilion itself, with its superbly spreading view over the vineyards, to take lunch at the Plaisance or Chez Germaine, with a St Emilion or a Pomerol to accompany the *entrecôte Bordelaise*, and a glass of Barsac or of Sauternes afterwards, with the macaroons that are the speciality of the little town.

Downstream from here, and on the opposite bank of the Gironde from the Médoc, are two similarly picturesque, but far less frequently visited towns, Bourg and Blaye – the latter, especially, still has impressive Vauban fortifications enclosing lawns on which it is agreeable to picnic and enjoy the river views.

There are good, drinkable red wines grown around here, of modest pretensions, but with a true claret quality, and the same can be said of the neighbouring districts of Cubzac and Fronsac.

Two more red Bordeaux regions remain to be mentioned (I omit some minor areas that will be found in the *appellation* list at the end of the chapter). One is minor in importance, one major.

The red wines of the Premières Côtes de Bordeaux, along the prettily wooded and steep right bank of the Garonne opposite the Graves, are dismissed curtly by Edmund Penning-Rowsell as 'ordinary' – but 'ordinary' in this part of France can be a good deal more pleasing than the 'ordinary' red wines of farther south.

Across the river, it is no longer true to say, as many books still do, that although everyone thinks of the Graves as white-wine country, it grows more reds. In fact, the production of red Graves is only about a quarter of the total, but its reds are much more distinguished than its whites, and some of the finest clarets of the region, with such growths as Domaine de Chevalier, Pape Clément, La Mission-Haut-Brion and others are well worth mentioning in the same breath as the first-growth Haut-Brion itself.

Of red Graves generally, it can be said that they are nearer to the Médocs than are the St Emilions and Pomerols. At their best, they can be superb, but on the more modest level that is what most of us can afford, I would choose a minor St Emilion rather than a minor Graves – it would be more forthcoming.

All this, though, is to judge by the highest standards in France – even when discussing minor wines and modest prices. The Bordelais in general, from the southernmost tip of the

Premières Côtes to the northernmost of the Médoc, is Tom Tiddler's ground to all who love French red wine.

The classification of the red wines of the Gironde, 1855

Châteaux	Communes
Premiers crus	
Lafite-Rothschild★	Pauillac
Margaux	Margaux
Latour	Pauillac
Haut-Brion	Pessac (Graves)
Deuxièmes crus	
Mouton-Rothschild	Pauillac
Rausan-Ségla	Margaux
Rauzan-Gassies	Margaux
Léoville-Las-Cases	Saint-Julien
Léoville-Poyferré	Saint-Julien
Léoville-Barton	Saint-Julien
Durfort-Vivens	Margaux
Gruaud-Larose	Saint-Julien
Lascombes	Margaux
Brane-Cantenac	Cantenac
Pichon-Longueville (Baron)	Pauillac
Pichon-Lalande	Pauillac
Ducru-Beaucaillou	Saint-Julien

★In 1973, the Minister of Agriculture endorsed a decision of the Bordeaux Chamber of Commerce to reclassify the First Growths, which are now entitled 'Premiers Crus Classés 1973' and are named in alphabetical order as follows:

> Château Lafite-Rothschild
> Château Latour
> Château Margaux
> Château Mouton Rothschild
> -par assimilation: Château Haut-Brion

| Cos d'Estournel | Saint-Estèphe |
| Montrose | Saint-Estèphe |

Troisièmes crus

Kirwan	Cantenac
Issan	Cantenac
Lagrange	Saint-Julien
Langoa-Barton	Saint-Julien
Giscours	Labarde
Malescot-Saint-Exupéry	Margaux
Cantenac-Brown	Cantenac
Boyd-Cantenac	Margaux
Palmer	Cantenac
La Lagune	Ludon
Desmirail	Margaux
Calon-Ségur	Saint-Estèphe
Ferrière	Margaux
Marquise d'Alesme-Becker	Margaux

Quatrièmes crus

Saint-Pierre-Sevaistre	Saint-Julien
Saint-Pierre-Bontemps	Saint-Julien
Talbot	Saint-Julien
Branaire-Ducru	Saint-Julien
Pouget	Cantenac
La Tour-Carnet	Saint-Laurent
Rochet	Saint-Estèphe
Beychevelle	Saint-Julien
Le Prieuré	Cantenac
Marquis-de-Terme	Margaux

Cinquièmes crus

Pontet-Canet	Pauillac
Batailley	Pauillac
Haut-Batailley	Pauillac

Grand-Puy-Lacoste	Pauillac
Grand-Puy-Ducasse	Pauillac
Lynch-Bages	Pauillac
Lynch-Moussas	Pauillac
Dauzac	Labarde
Mouton-Baron Phillippe	Pauillac
Le Tertre	Arsac
Haut-Bages-Libéral	Pauillac
Pédesclaux	Pauillac
Belgrave	Saint-Laurent
Camensac	Saint-Laurent
Cos-Labory	Saint-Estèphe
Clerc-Milon	Pauillac
Croizet-Bages	Pauillac
Cantemerle	Macau

THE WINES OF BORDEAUX

All these wines are AOC.

Barsac

One of the five *communes* entitled to the *appellation* 'Sauternes', and the only one entitled to its own as an alternative. It is quite the biggest of the five, and although its ordinary *commune* wine can be very ordinary sweet stuff, without much depth or delicacy, its two leading growths, Château Coutet and Château Climens (pronounce the final 's') are in the same class as the great Yquem – nearer in quality and breed, at any rate, than the big difference in price would indicate.

Blaye or Blayais

Both reds and whites, and single-vineyard wines of either are worth seeking out, though I consider the reds better. Edmund Penning-Rowsell writes warmly of the countryside of this right bank of the Gironde, the good value of its restaurants (it is a region little visited by foreigners) and of the red wines of Blaye, Bourg, Fronsac and Cubzac that they are 'the essential red Bordeaux which for centuries have helped to build the reputation of claret'. He counsels giving them bottle-age.

Bordeaux
Bordeaux Clairet
Bordeaux Rosé
Bordeaux Supérieur
Bordeaux Supérieur Clairet
Bordeaux Supérieur Rosé

The generic term for red and white wines from anywhere in the region, and of wines from one part and another are entitled only to this widest of *appellations*.

Thus a wine labelled 'Bordeaux Appellation Contrôlée' can be either the most modest offering of the most modest vigneron on the edge of the Bordelais, observing the minimum requirements of the rules for *appellation*, or it can be a bottle of Mouton Cadet, bearing a vintage year, made by the people who make Mouton itself, and commanding quite a high price, but not entitled to an inner *appellation* because according to the balance of the vintage, some St Emilion or some Fronsac or some Blaye will be blended with the basic Pauillac.

Much simple Bordeaux comes from cooperatives, and very good it can be. I have seen for myself how well worth while it is to put even the cheapest Bordeaux Rouge away for a few months or a year to give it bottle-age.

The clairet (from which we derive our word 'claret') and the rosé are the same thing: '*supérieur*' indicates a degree more alcoholic strength. This does not necessarily mean high quality, but it usually does, and gives greater staying power.

Bordeaux Mousseux
A certain amount of sparkling wine is made in the region, but in my experience the Bordelais drink champagne.

Bordeaux Haut-Benauge
Medium-sweet white wines from a corner of the Entre-Deux-Mers considered worthy of its own *appellation*: not worth a detour.

Bordeaux Côtes-de-Castillon
Bordeaux Supérieur Côtes-de-Castillon
Red wines ('*supérieur*' equals 'stronger') from around the town where, in 1453, the English lost a battle and the region of Aquitaine. They are near to St Emilion both geographically and in style – a bottle in a local restaurant that looks after its wine would be cheaper than a St Emilion, and very good value.

Bordeaux Côtes-de-Francs
Bordeaux Supérieur Côtes-de-Francs
Reds and whites from a very small area just to the north of the Côtes-de-Castillon (see above). I have not tasted them and they are not mentioned even in Edmund Penning-Rowsell's monumental work. The reds must be very like the Castillons.

Bourg or Bourgeais
Reds and whites from the right bank of the Gironde: see under Blaye. The Bourg wines are a little fuller than those of Blaye, but there is little to choose.

Cadillac
The quality of the reds and whites from around this interesting little walled town is not quite so high as that of the American motor-car.

Fair reds and whites are produced. It is the white Cadillac that is entitled to the *appellation*. Some of the sweet whites are better value than the cheaper Barsacs and Sauternes, from just across the river.

Cérons
From hard by the Sauternais, the white wines of Cérons are made in the same way from the same grapes as Sauternes and Barsac.

Never quite so luscious, I consider them delicious with fruit or even, sometimes, with a creamy cheese. Yet I am told that they are hard to sell abroad because, as Alexis Lichine puts it, they are neither so dry as a dry Graves nor so sweet as Sauternes.

Côtes Canon-Fronsac or Canon-Fronsac
Hearty, fruity red wines, rather like sound St Emilions, from the other side of the busy little town of Libourne. Considered slightly superior to Côtes de Fronsac, though I find little to choose.

Côtes de Bourg
Côtes de Blaye
Reds and whites, see under Blaye: 'Côtes de' indicates slightly more rigorous restriction as to yield per acre, and slightly higher strength.

Côtes de Bordeaux Saint-Macaire
Medium-sweet white wines from the Entre-Deux-Mers: they lack the savour of the Cérons (q.v.).

Côtes de Fronsac
See under Côtes Canon-Fronsac, above.

Entre-Deux-Mers

Dryish or sweetish white wines from the vast stretch between the Garonne and the Dordogne: the best of them have *appellations* of their own, and are richer. (See under Cadillac, Loupiac and Sainte-Croix-du-Mont.) The dry qualifies for the *appellation* 'Entre-Deux-Mers', the sweet only for 'Bordeaux'.

Entre-Deux-Mers-Haut-Benauge

See under Bordeaux Haut-Benauge: I know of no difference.

Graves
Graves Supérieures

The differences are that the *appellation* Graves applies to both reds and whites, the *appellation* Graves Supérieures to whites only, and these a degree the stronger in alcohol.

For the reds and whites in general, see the introductory paragraphs to this chapter (pages 151 and 158).

Graves-de-Vayres

A small north-eastern corner of the Entre-deux-Mers that produces a sort of poor man's white Graves.

Haut-Médoc

'*Haut*' means here upstream, or higher up the river.

The triangular peninsula of the Médoc grows wine in its eastern half, and better wine in the southern two-thirds of this, from Bordeaux to just beyond St Estèphe, than in the other third, from St Estèphe to the Pointe de Grave.

So the *appellation* Haut-Médoc is a cut above the *appellation* Médoc, *tout court* (it used to be Bas-Médoc, meaning merely 'downstream Médoc', but this was objected to by the natives).

The finer wines of the Médoc are those entitled to one or other of the six *commune appellations* – Margaux, Moulis,

Listrac, Pauillac, Saint-Julien and Saint-Estèphe and, within these, the best of all carry their château names, though these are not in themselves *appellations*.

Even a Médoc or Haut-Médoc *appellation*, though, should indicate a red wine of true claret style. At their worst, as I have observed in the introduction to this chapter, they can be sharp and thin, but one is often very pleasantly surprised by the quality of a mere carafe wine at one of the little restaurants of the region (which are not themselves very good).

Lalande de Pomerol

Red wine from a region that adjoins the grander Pomerol region itself: Edmund Penning-Rowsell considers its wines coarser and less subtle than the Pomerols, but guesses, cynically, that many are sold as such.

Listrac

One of the six *communes* of the Haut-Médoc (q.v.). None of its wines is a classified growth, but some of the *bourgeois* growths are good, tough wines that age well in bottle. The one I know is Fourcas-Hosten, sometimes to be found in British wine-merchants' lists.

Loupiac

A sweet white wine from near Cadillac, across the river from Barsac, and very like that of Cadillac itself.

Lussac-Saint-Emilion

A *commune* of St Emilion; it might well be assumed that a bottle bearing this *appellation* would be a cut above one entitled only to the ordinary *appellation* St Emilion, but the contrary is the case.

Anyway, a full red claret, rather bigger and blander than a Médoc.

Margaux

One of the six named *communes* of the Haut-Médoc and one of the finest, with Château Margaux, a first growth (which must not be confused with the *commune appellation*), as its pride and joy, but with nine other *crus classés* and a number of other, minor, single-vineyard wines.

Soft, delicate and fragrant, even a *commune* wine with the bare *appellation* is one of the world's finer red wines.

Médoc

See under Haut-Médoc, above.

Montagne-Saint-Emilion

One of the individually named *communes* of St Emilion: see under Lussac-Saint-Emilion, above.

Moulis
Moulis-en-Médoc

One of the six named *communes* of the Haut-Médoc, but not so grand as Margaux, Pauillac, St Julien or St Estèphe.

There are no *crus classés*, but Chasse-Spleen – splendid name for a wine! – is a *grand cru exceptionnel*, and a fine, full-bodied claret that takes a good deal of ageing. Edmund Penning-Rowsell thinks highly, too, of the Dutruch-Grand-Poujeaux, easier to drink than to pronounce.

Néac

Adjoins, and is precisely similar to, Lalande-de-Pomerol, see above.

Parsac-Saint-Emilion

A named individual *commune* of St Emilion, like Lussac (q.v.).

Pauillac

One of the six named *communes* of the Haut-Médoc, and the most distinguished, for it includes more *cru classé* growths –

eighteen – than any other *commune*, and no fewer than three of the five first growths – Lafite, Latour and Mouton.

No other *commune* has more than one.

Generally speaking, the wines of Pauillac are lighter than those of St Estèphe, to the north; less light than those of St Julien and Margaux, to the south.

But this *is* to speak generally: within the *commune* much depends on the proportions of the grapes grown and the methods of vinification – Mouton and Latour are bigger, harder wines than Lafite.

Such wines as bear the simple *appellation* are, along with the St Juliens, as near to being archetypal clarets as one can hope to taste.

Pomerol

A tiny area, north and north-east of Libourne, adjoining the much bigger St Emilion region, the wines of which are very similar.

Soft, full, 'immediately attractive', to use Edmund Penning-Rowsell's phrase, these are delicious clarets.

Châteaux Petrus and Vieux Château Certan command prices similar to those paid for first growths of the Médoc but, because the area is so small, simple Pomerol, entitled only to the bare *commune appellation*, can be quite delicious, and I would choose it in preference to any other wine of the Bordelais with only a *commune appellation*. I have never been disappointed in even the most modest Pomerol.

Premières Côtes de Blaye

Slightly superior reds and whites of Blaye (q.v.) – smaller permitted yield and higher alcoholic strength.

Premières Côtes de Bordeaux

Reds and whites from the right bank of the Garonne between

Langon and Bordeaux. There are some sound reds and some good sweet whites, the best of both of which are entitled to hyphenate the name of their *communes*: there are nearly forty of these and, in turn, the very best of that lot, such as Cadillac (q.v.) may use their own individual names without hyphenating.

Puisseguin Saint-Emilion
Sables Saint-Emilion
Named individual *communes* of Saint-Emilion: see under Lussac.

Sainte Croix-du-Mont
One of the richer, fuller, sweeter white wines of Entre-Deux-Mers. See under Cadillac and Loupiac.

Saint-Emilion
Saint-Emilion Grand Cru
Saint-Emilion Grand Cru Classé
Saint-Emilion Premier Grand Cru Classé
A bigger region even than the Médoc, producing some of the greatest of all clarets – Cheval Blanc and Ausone among them – and, in general, what Hugh Johnson describes as 'claret moving towards burgundy, full, savoury and strong'.

The wines of this most attractive countryside mature more quickly than those of the Graves and the Médoc, and should be that much cheaper. If they are not, it is because they are so much sought after, and with good reason; they are among the easiest to like and to understand of all fine French red wines.

Saint-Estèphe
Northernmost of the six named *communes* of the Médoc, and producing the biggest and hardest wines. Not quite so immediately appealing as those of St Julien, Pauillac and

Margaux, they are sound wines to put away, and such *cru classés* as Montrose and Cos d'Estournel at their best are generous and heart-warming. But on the *commune appellation* level I prefer a St Emilion or a Pomerol, from across the river, or a St Julien from this side.

Sainte-Foy-Bordeaux
Reds and whites from the Entre-Deux-Mers (q.v.).

Saint-Georges-Saint-Emilion
See under Lussac.

Saint-Julien
Of the six named *communes* in the Haut-Médoc, this lies more or less in the middle.

I know that there cannot be a middle one of six, which is why I write 'more or less', but the firmer Pauillacs grow to the north, the softer Margaux to the south, and St Julien, though it has no first-growth château, can boast no fewer than eleven other *crus classés* and produces what Edmund Penning-Rowsell in his classic book on Bordeaux, has described as, at its best, 'the quintessence of claret'.

Unfortunately, it is so sought after that the producer of any wine that can scrape into the *appellation* qualification for St Julien, however run of the mill, will demand a high price: I have enjoyed some of the *crus classés* of St Julien more than most – Léoville-Barton and Beychevelle in particular – but I have sometimes been disappointed in a simple St Julien and wished that I had chosen a Pomerol or St Emilion.

Sauternes
See preliminary paragraphs of this chapter, and under Barsac. As has already been explained, the *commune* of Sauternes gives its name to the A O C wines of four other *communes*. Two of the

most distinguished, Coutet and Climens, come in fact from Barsac. But the greatest of all sweet white wines comes from Sauternes itself – Château d'Yquem, usually referred to simply as Yquem.

When the sweet white wines of the region were graded in 1955 into two classes, a special category was created for Yquem alone – *premier grand cru* – in recognition of its prestige and the much greater price it commanded than did its closest rivals.

Other noble Sauternes besides the three already named are Suduiraut, Rieussec and Guiraud. Many people prefer such wines, finding the richness of Yquem almost too much of a good thing.

For Reference

A list of all the named wines of the region is in:

COCKS, CHARLES, and FÉRET, EDOUARD, *Bordeaux et Ses Vins*, Bordeaux, 1969.

For Further Reading

PENNING-ROWSELL, EDMUND, *The Wines of Bordeaux*, fourth edition, Penguin, 1976.
RAY, CYRIL, *Lafite*, Peter Davies, 1968.
RAY, CYRIL, *Mouton-Rothschild*, Christie Wine Publications, 1974.

The Loire

THE long and lovely river Loire links wine-growing areas as far apart as the Massif Central and the shores of the Atlantic – from those of Saint-Pourçain and Pouilly-sur-Loire, looking on the map as though they should be regarded as burgundies, by way of vineyards around Bourges, around Gien and around Orleans, to the seaside Muscadet.

In spite of differences between the various regions, spread out as they are over five hundred miles of France, and more – differences of soils, of grape varieties, of ways of life and of micro-climates – there is a sort of family resemblance between all the Loire wines.

Partly, at any rate, this is because they are northern wines: along with Champagne, Burgundy and the Rhine Mosel region, this is getting on for as far north as wine can be grown economically on a big scale.

Northern wines have a lightness and freshness deriving from an acidity that balances their fruitiness. At their worst, they can be thin, just as the wines from warmer climates, at *their* worst, are coarse or flabby. At their best, though, they are graceful and refreshing, and many (as in Champagne) tend to retain a slight effervescence, or to renew it during the spring after the vintage, because winter comes too soon for the first fermentation to complete itself.

Another factor in the family resemblance of the Loire wines, most of which are white, is the predominance of the Sauvignon grape.

It is used, along with the Chardonnay and others, in the

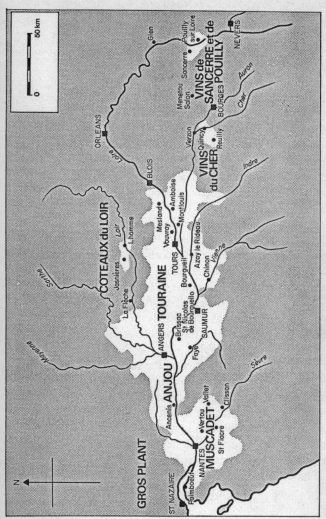

Map II. The Loire

173

making of Saint-Pourçain, the Loire wine furthest from the sea – grown on the banks of the Sioule, tributary of a Loire tributary, in the heart of the Cevennes, not far from Vichy, the cure at which is sometimes said to owe as much to the dry, apple-crisp wine as to the spa's alkaline waters.

Sauvignon, too, for the more famous Pouilly Fumé (not to be confused with Burgundy's Pouilly Fuissé), downstream on the Loire itself, the clean, fresh wine with the flavour, says Morton Shand, of gun-flint, to which Pamela Vandyke Price replies,* 'how many of us have tasted gun-flints?' – going on, though, to observe of the Sancerre from over the river, also a Sauvignon wine, that it 'can smell like a mountain meadow when the snows are melting, cool but with a floweriness in the background'.

There is a pocket of dry, white AOC wines west of here, on the Cher, around Quincy and Reuilly, and red and white VDQS wines are grown around Gien and around Orleans, none of which need delay our reaching Blois, and the beginning of the great stretch of the noblest of Loire wines.

From here more than half-way to the sea, it is château-country – according to Edward Hyams 'about the most fatly satisfying, and in places the lovelist countryside in Europe, not excluding England'.†

The princes and noblemen of the French High Renaissance chose to build their palaces here because of the luminous skies, the benign, temperate climate, the game, the grape – and other fruits, too, from that time to this: this is a land of orchards as well as of vineyards, and in the Boulevard du Roi René in Angers a plaque commemorates the raising in 1849–50 of the celebrated pear, Doyenné du Comice.

That is in the heart of Anjou, though, and before we reach

*Pamela Vandyke Price, *Eating and Drinking in France Today* (Tom Stacey, 1972).
†Edward Hyams, *Vin* (Newnes, 1959).

so far downstream there are the wines of Touraine, of which the best-known are the Vouvrays – dry and sweet, still and sparkling. The sparklers are a hint softer and fruitier than the classic champagnes, though made in the same way, and to many people that much more acceptable, especially as they are cheaper, literally into the bargain.

The grape here is the Chénin Blanc, and its wines are remarkable among French whites in their capacity for ageing.

A little downstream is the one area in the Loire noted for its red wines – an area straddling the river, with Chinon, Rabelais's birthplace, on the left bank (in fact, on the Vienne, a tributary) and Bourgueil on the right.

These two names are carried by red wines made from the grape called in these parts the Breton, but which is the Cabernet Franc of Bordeaux and, especially, of St Emilion, to the wines of which they bear a family resemblance.

Edward Hyams said that Chinon and Bourgeuil are identical; Robin Yapp says that they are similar, but that Chinon is perhaps somewhat the softer. They mature well in the cellars tunnelled into the chalk cliffs that front the river (this is troglodytic country: some caves are houses; some houses are half-caves) and they show well when served cool, like young Beaujolais.

There is a small outlying wine-growing region to the north, on the masculine Loir, as distinct from the feminine Loire, to which it is tributary: its reds and its whites are pleasant drinking on the spot, especially to lovers of the French classic writers, whom they can quote as they quaff – Ronsard wrote verses in their honour, and Rabelais rubbed his hands with glee to recall that the sleepy little country town of La Chartre-sur-le-Loir, which even to this day numbers fewer than two thousand souls, was full in his time of wine-merchants and boasted at least twenty-seven inn-keepers.

Back to the Loire itself, and downstream to the pink wines

of Anjou, fragrant and sweet or sweetish – the best of them made from the Cabernet grape, as are the infrequent reds. The rosés are often stronger than they look. The dry rosé of the region carries the new *appellation* Rosé de la Loire.

Here, too, is Saumur, an elegant city of horses and horsemen – home of the French army's school of equitation, and of the Cadre Noir, which is France's equivalent of the white-horse Spanish Riding School of Vienna.

The pinks of Saumur in particular are drier than those of Anjou in general; the white Saumur sparklers have more of the juice of black grapes in them than those of Vouvray, and are therefore more full-bodied.

Downstream, west of Angers, the river Layon runs into the Loire, and along its banks are grown some of France's most delightful sweet dessert wines. Of the sweet Coteaux du Layon wines, those of the Quarts de Chaume are the best-known (which does not mean that they are well-known) and Bonnezeaux probably the best, and hardly known at all in Britain, save to customers of Yapp of Mere. They are made either after the grapes have been attacked by the noble rot, like those of Sauternes or, if the weather does not conduce to the rot setting in, after they have withered, raisin-like, on the vine.

They are full in flavour and high in alcohol, yet always seem fresher and less cloying than their grander rivals from the Sauternais – their underlying acidity makes them more closely resemble the great sweet Mosels.

Big white wines come also from the Coteaux de la Loire, downstream again, and on the other side of the river, north of Nantes. They are medium dry, brimming with flavour, and although difficult to match with food – too dry for fruit, too fruity and fragrant to go well with savoury dishes, like many German wines – they are too delicious to ignore. Perhaps Hugh Johnson's is the right answer: 'really more enjoyable quite divorced from any meal at all, when you are simply sitting at a table by the river with legs outstretched and time to think'.*

Two vineyards in the Coteaux, Coulée de Serrant and La Roche-aux-Moines, produce the most expensive of all the Loire wines, and their names are bracketed with that of Savennières, in the Coteaux, and given *appellations* of their own. The appropriately-named Madame Joly owns one, and part of the other.

Then, at last, to the great spread of Muscadet vineyards, fanning out on either side of the river, and of Nantes, almost to the once-embattled beaches of St Nazaire. The best and the most come from the more inland part of the region, along the Sèvre, and have the *appellation* Sèvre et Maine.

Little-known even up to the late nineteen-twenties, when Morton Shand could write that 'it is very popular in Nantes, and has rather surprisingly latterly acquired a considerable reputation throughout France and even in other countries', Muscadet has become, like Beaujolais and (outside France) Yugoslav Riesling, a sort of basic swigging wine for meals at home, as wine by the glass, and in modest restaurants. By the nineteen-fifties Raymond Postgate was observing that it had 'risen almost too rapidly into popularity'.†

It is, as John Arlott has written of Beaujolais,‡ a drinking-man's wine, to be drunk deep of, not sipped, and as a true thirst-quencher.

The best, to earn a Muscadet *appellation*, is made of the grape it is named after, which is a sort – but quite what sort I do not know; nor does anyone else for that matter – of the Gamay of Burgundy, and there is a rather drier, but less

*Hugh Johnson, *Wine* (Nelson, 1960).

†Raymond Postgate, *The Plain Man's Guide to Wine* (Michael Joseph, 1951).

‡In an article in the *Guardian*.

distinguished wine of the region, with a VDQS of its own, made from the Gros Plant. As Muscadet has become more expensive, so Gros Plant has become more widely planted, and better-known.

Both wines are drunk well-chilled, and go splendidly with fish, as well they should in this paradise for fish-eaters. Again, like Beaujolais, they are drunk young and fresh, and just as there is something of a vogue for Beaujolais Nouveau, or Beaujolais Primeur, so there is for the similarly young Muscadet-sur-lie.

This is a Muscadet bottled in the early spring after the vintage, but direct from the wood it has fermented in and thus straight off the '*lie*' or sediment, instead of having previously been 'racked' from one cask to another, as is usual, in order to leave sediment behind.

According to Robin Yapp, the wine 'seems to gain some quality from its prolonged contact with the sediment, and is fuller, rounder, and fruitier'. (Although one is a young and cheapish wine, the other oldish and expensive, there is an obvious comparison to be made between Muscadet-sur-lie and the Bollinger RD champagne: both gain their character from the prolonged contact with the lees.) It has to be bottled carefully because of possible cloudiness or a renewed fermentation in bottle, but the odd few crystals that sometimes form in the bottom of the bottle are of no importance, and the slight prickle of secondary fermentation can be refreshing.

THE WINES OF THE LOIRE
AOC

Anjou
The *appellation* applies to red, white and rosé wines, though the rosé may also style itself 'Rosé d'Anjou: appellation contrôlée' (see below).

The rosé – which is sweet or semi-sweet – is by far the best-known, and the permitted production per hectare is greater than that for the white, which in turn is greater than for the red.

For their relative styles and merits, see introductory paragraphs to this chapter (page 176).

Anjou Coteaux de la Loire
An *appellation* solely for better quality sweet or semi-sweet rosé, made only from Cabernet Franc and Cabernet Sauvignon grapes, and with a lower permitted production per hectare than the simple Anjou rosé.

Anjou Pétillant
Semi-sparkling, white or rosé: flavoury, but not high in alcohol – a refreshing picnic wine.

Anjou Mousseux
White, champagne method, but fuller in flavour than champagne: sparkling Saumur would be entitled to this *appellation* but is more restricted, and of higher quality.

Blanc Fumé de Pouilly or Pouilly Fumé
See introductory paragraphs: a clean, flavoury, distinctive white wine, similar to Sancerre (q.v.) from the other side of the upper reaches of the river.

Pouilly or Pouilly-sur-Loire is the name of the town, and some of its wines, made from the Chasselas grape, or a blend of Chasselas and Sauvignon, are entitled to that *appellation* only: to be Pouilly-Fumé the wine has to be made exclusively from the Sauvignon grape.

As Pouilly-Fumé commands the higher price, the Chasselas is giving ground to the Sauvignon. Wine from individual vineyards also sells better than the cooperative wines: Château du Nozet has long been a favourite in Britain.

Bourgueil

Along with Chinon, one of the two really distinctive red wines of what is largely a white-wine and rosé region.

Made from the Cabernet Franc of Bordeaux and, more particularly, of St Emilion, the wines of which it resembles though showing, to my mind (or, rather, to my nose) a prettier flowery scent.

It ages well, though I would not quarrel with those who enjoy it young and cooled, like a young Beaujolais.

Bonnezeaux

An inner *appellation* of Coteaux du Layon, for one of the most delicious of naturally sweet white wines – less heavily luscious than those of the Sauternais, and possibly a shade more fragrant than the very similar Quarts de Chaume.

Cabernet d'Anjou

The best of the region's red and sweet or semi-sweet rosé wines – see under Anjou Coteaux de la Loire. The reds – not so frequent as the rosés – are particularly light and easy to drink.

Not to be taken so seriously as clarets, from the same grape but, by the same token, perhaps to be taken all the more freely.

Chinon

See under Bourgueil. Experts, but not I, can detect a difference between the two red wines.

Coteaux de l'Aubance

Light, very pretty, sweetish white wine from near the château town of Brissac – seldom met with elsewhere.

Coteaux du Layon

Less distinguished than the above, which has an inner, more restricted, *appellation*, these are the fullish, usually quite sweet, white wines from the whole valley of the Layon, which runs into the Loire below Angers.

The top growths of this area have their own *appellations*: Quarts de Chaume and Bonnezeaux are the aristocrats, but any of the following *commune* names bracketed with the generic *appellation* will indicate a quality above average:

Beaulieu-sur-Layon	Rochefort
Faye-d'Anjou	Saint-Lambert-du-Lattay
Rablay-sur-Layon	Chaume
Saint-Aubin-de-Luigné	

Coteaux du Loir

Note the difference in spelling between Loir, the tributary, and Loire, the main stream.

Reds, whites and rosés are grown, and under fairly severe restrictions as to yield and type of grape.

Morton Shand claimed that the reds 'have a rather individual flavour', which can mean anything – indeed, the imagination overstrains itself.

For myself, I observe that the region lies outside the main area of the Loire, and I consider only one of its wines '*vaut le voyage*' or even, in Monsieur Michelin's other marmoreal phrase, '*mérite un détour*', and that is not one of Shand's rather individual reds, but the delicious white Jasnières (see below).

Coteaux de Saumur

Dry and sweetish white wines from the chalky hills south of the town itself: it may be the chalk that makes the dry wine of this district seem to me to resemble a still champagne.

Jasnières

A rare white wine from the otherwise undistinguished Coteaux du Loir (q.v.) but resembling a good Vouvray or a better Montlouis in its medium-sweet fullness and honey-like scent. Resembles a good hock in being ideal for drinking by itself on a summer's evening rather than with a meal.

Menetou-Salon

A dry white from between Bourges and Sancerre, similar in style to Sancerre and Pouilly-Fumé, but perhaps more flowery to the nose than either.

Montlouis

One of the great sweet whites of Vouvray, if not reaching perhaps quite such heights as Quarts de Chaume and Bonnezeaux (qq.v.).

There are also sparkling and semi-sparkling versions, which I do not rate so high:

Montlouis Pétillant
Montlouis Mousseux.

Muscadet

Ah, now we come to one of the greatest wines of France – not 'greatest' in the sense of high quality but of importance as a beverage. Muscadet is 'great' in the same way that bread or rice is 'great' – it matters a great deal to a great number of people. It would be impossible, but how fascinating, to know how many dozen oysters have been washed down by how many glasses of Muscadet.

For more on the subject, see opening paragraphs of this chapter (pages 177–8), which deal also with Muscadet de Sèvre-et-de-Maine.

Muscadet des Coteaux de la Loire
Indistinguishable, save geographically – the list of *communes* is different – from the Muscadet de Sèvre-et-de-Maine.

Muscadet de Sèvre-et-Maine
See under Muscadet, above.

Pouilly-sur-Loire
Not quite so elegant as the Pouilly-Fumé: for the differences, see under Blanc Fumé de Pouilly, above.

Pouilly Fumé de Pouilly or Pouilly Fumé
Also see under Blanc Fumé de Pouilly, above.

Quarts-de-Chaumes
Along with Bonnezeaux (q.v.) one of the fine, naturally sweet wines of the region. See introductory paragraphs of this chapter (page 176).

Quincy
Little-known in Britain, and yet the second *vignoble* in France to be accorded an *appellation contrôlée*, only three months after Châteauneuf du Pape, in 1936.

A dry, yet fruitily mouth-filling Sauvignon white wine, from near Bourges, and not unlike the Sancerre and the Pouilly-Fumé from just the other side of that (by French standards) rather boring town.

Reuilly
A very small production, from a very small area, virtually an extension of Quincy (see above), from the white wines of which its own white it virtually indistinguishable. There is a red, rather like a Beaujolais, and a rosé that is neither here nor there.

Rosé d'Anjou
Rosé d'Anjou Pétillant
See under Anjou, above.

All Anjou rosés must have a natural grape-sugar content of at least 10 grams per litre.

Rosé de Loire
A very new *appellation*, made public in December 1974. From this date, the *appellation* Rosé d'Anjou and Cabernet d'Anjou Rosé apply only to the sweet pinks of the region. Rosé de la Loire is the pink wine of Anjou and Touraine that has been fully fermented out and is quite dry.

Saint-Nicolas-de-Bourgueil
An inner *appellation* of Bourgueil itself (q.v.) – yield per hectare is more limited, and I suppose that a wine with this label is a cut above Bourgueil, but much would depend on the grower, and on how the wine would be kept. Good stuff, anyway.

Sancerre
A fine, flavoury Sauvignon white wine, very similar to – to me, indistinguishable from – the Pouilly Fumé from across the river. See introductory paragraphs to this chapter (page 174).

Savennières
Fine, medium-dry white wines, full of fragrance and of flavour, from north of Nantes – see introductory paragraphs to this chapter (page 177). The two finest each have a hyphenated *appellation*:

Savennières-Coulée-de-Serrant
Savennières-Roches-aux-Moines.

Saumur
Red and white wines both qualify for the *appellation*, but this is a country of white wines, which resemble those entitled to be called 'Anjou' and 'Coteaux-de-Saumur' (qq.v.). There are sparkling and semi-sparkling whites:

> Saumur Pétillant
> Saumur Mousseux,

for the latter of which see the introductory paragraphs to this chapter (page 176).

Touraine
Reds, whites and rosés; still, sparkling and pétillant wines can all qualify for this *appellation*, the whites quite the most frequently met with. It is well to look for the more restricted *appellations*, such as Chinon and Bourgueil for the reds and Vouvray for the whites, of which Touraine, *tout simple*, is a poor relation.

Rather finer qualities may carry the inner *appellations*:

> Touraine Amboise
> Touraine Azay-le-Rideau
> Touraine Mesland

or be sparkling or semi-sparkling:

> Touraine Pétillant
> Touraine Mousseux.

Vouvray
A cut above 'Touraine' as an *appellation*, and a cut below its own such inner *appellations* as Quarts-de-Chaume. There are also, of course:

> Vouvray Pétillant
> Vouvray Mousseux.

VDQS

With so many Loire wines entitled to AOC status, one must not expect too much of the VDQS wines of the region. They are:

Châteaumeillant
Coteaux de Châteaumeillant
Red, white and rosé (or *vin gris*) wines are made in this small district near Sancerre: I have never come across any of them.

Cheverny
Cour-Cheverny
Mont-Près-Chambord
Valençay
These are in the official list of VDQS wines, but I cannot find them in any reference books, nor have I ever met them.

Coteaux d'Ancenis
On the edge of the spreading Muscadet region is the pleasant little town of Ancenis, some couple of dozen miles upstream from Nantes. Around it some drinkable modest red and white wines are made – all necessarily with the name of the informing grape bracketed with the regional name:

Pineau de la Loire	Pinot-Beurot
Chenin Blanc	Gamay
Malvoisie	Cabernet

The Pineau and the Cabernet are worth looking out for, as local wines.

Coteaux du Vendômois
White wines from near Vendôme, and not worth seeking out farther afield.

Côtes d'Auvergne
Vins d'Auvergne

These red, white and rosé wines hardly deserve to be regarded as Loire wines at all – neither in style nor geographically.

They come from the lower slopes of the Massif Central, towards Moulins and Clermont-Ferrand which, as Vivian Rowe says, produces wines that are 'hard and not all that well flavoured'.*

Côtes du Forez

Red and rosé: see Côtes d'Auvergne, above.

Gros Plant
Gros Plant du Pays Nantais

A useful, and plentiful, white wine from the Muscadet region but not made of the Muscadet grape. Drier and less distinguished than Muscadet itself, but good with shellfish.

Vin des Coteaux du Giennois
Côtes de Gien

Red and white wines, very light, both in style and in alcohol, from around Gien, which is between Sancerre and Orleans.

Vin du Haut-Poitou

These undistinguished wines come from the southern edge of the westernmost regions of the Loire – south of the Muscadet and Saumur countries and on the way to Cognac. They are of no importance.

Vin de l'Orléanais

Some very pleasant red wines come from north of Orleans: I have met them only in the restaurants of that city, where I

*Vivian Rowe, *French Wines, Ordinary and Extraordinary* (Harrap, 1972).

have much enjoyed them. But they are not swagger wines to be sought out elsewhere.

Côte Roannaise

Reds and rosés from what is almost Rhône rather than Loire country. Very low in alcohol. They may be found at the cheaper end of the lists in the starred restaurants of Renaison (the Jacques Cœur) and Roanne (the very famous Frères Troisgros) but they are not in the same class as the grub.

Vin de Saint-Pourçain-sur-Sioule

This might soon, on merit, move up from VDQS to AOC status – a dry, clean white wine, served in most of the restaurants of Vichy, near which spa it is grown. Red and rosé wine is entitled to the *appellation*, too, but it is the white that I am enthusiastic about.

Vin de Thouarsais

A lesser wine of the area of Quarts-de-Chaume (q.v.).

Valençay

From the Touraine region, south-west of Blois: I have never seen any.

For Further Reading

ROWE, VIVIAN, *French Wines, Ordinary and Extraordinary*, Harrap, 1972.

WOON, BASIL, *The Big Little Wines of France*, Wine & Spirit Trade Publications, 1972.

YAPP BROTHERS of Mere, Wiltshire, *Current* [Twice-yearly] *Price-Lists* (by application).

CHAPTER 12

Vins Doux Naturels, Vins de Liqueur and Vermouth

THE list submitted by the French Ministry of Agriculture to the EEC in September 1973, referred to in my preface, ends with an apparently arbitrary couple of sections, one consisting of eighteen wines headed 'Vins Doux Naturels' (VDN) – 'Natural Sweet Wines' – and the other of five 'Vins de Liqueur' (VDL) – 'Liqueur Wines'.

I call the lists arbitrary – or apparently arbitrary – for two reasons. It is difficult to understand why, for example, a naturally sweet, which is to say unfortified, wine such as Barsac or Sauternes is listed under 'Bordeaux' and not in this separate list, whereas a sweet wine such as Beaumes de Venise appears here, also described as naturally sweet, and not among its fellows of the Rhône.

The reason for this seeming anomaly is that what the French describe as natural sweet wines are not in fact 'natural' in the true sense of the word. A VDN wine, such as Beaumes de Venise, is permitted fortification by the addition of 5 to 10 per cent of alcohol by volume. A Sauternes or a Barsac is permitted no such fortification and, however sweet, remains listed with the truly natural wines, however dry, of its own region.

The other oddity is that three wines – or one wine under three names: Frontignan, Muscat de Frontignan and Vin de Frontignan – appear under both headings, as Vins Doux Naturels and as Vins de Liqueur.

Here, the reason is that the two types of sweet wine differ

in the amount of fortification, and in the method of production.

The 'natural' wines have to be made from freshly fermented juice and the limited amount of alcohol that is permitted must be added during fermentation.

The 'liqueur' wines may include concentrates as well as freshly fermented juice; the alcohol may be added after as well as during fermentation, and in a greater proportion than for the 'natural' wines; a further 3 per cent by volume of natural brandies or rum 'to give bouquet and fragrance'. The resultant wine must be, and is, of greater alcoholic strength than a 'natural' wine.

The explanation for the appearance of Frontignan under both headings is that in that area, near Montpellier, the basic Muscat wine is treated in both ways.

VDN wines may be sold without *appellation* – many, indeed, are sold under brand names, like other apéritifs and dessert wines – but in practice those that are not branded carry the *appellations* they are entitled to, for no VDN wine is accepted by INAO unless it comes from a demarcated area and is made from a prescribed grape (Grenache, Muscat, Maccabeo or Malvoisie).

The only VDL wine with an *appellation* all its own is Pineau des Charentes (see below).

Finally, a word about vermouth, which is wine flavoured with herbs, spices and barks, and fortified with spirit to the strength approximately of sherry. (The name comes from the German *vermut*, wormwood, which used to be, but no longer is, an ingredient.)

Marseilles is the main centre of French vermouth manufacture, as Turin is of Italian, but the old distinction between French, dry, and Italian, sweet, no longer obtains: all French and all Italian firms make dry and sweet vermouths – usually sweet red, dry white and sweet white.

Most French vermouths are sold under their makers' or their brand names: only one has an *appellation* of its own – Chambéry, from the town of that name in Savoy, in the foothills of the Alps, the mountain herbs of which flavour the dry, delicate white vermouth. There is no red and no sweet Chambéry, but one of the two leading firms of the town makes a pale-pink, slightly sweeter version, known as Chambéryzette, flavoured with the juice of wild strawberries.

VINS DOUX NATURELS

Banyuls or Banyuls Grand Cru
Made from the Grenache grape in the eastern Pyrenean foothills, almost on the Spanish frontier.

Banyuls Rancio
The same sweet wine, after it has become maderized, when it is enjoyed by the locals, but not by me.

Côtes d'Agly
Côtes du Haut-Roussillon
Sweet VDN and VDL Muscat wines – red, white and rosé – similar to all the other Muscats of Roussillon.

Frontignan
A sweet Muscat from the Mediterranean coast near Montpellier. Both VDN and the stronger VDL wines are made: see below.

Grand Roussillon
Grand Roussillon Rancio
From just north of Banyuls (q.v.) but different in style – more fragrant – because made not from the Grenache, but from the Muscat grape. For the Rancio the comments on the Banyuls Rancio apply.

Maury
Maury Rancio
From the mountainous region inland from Perpignan; a wine that has not come my way, but I gather it resembles the other Muscats of the region. For the Rancio, see above.

Muscat de Beaumes de Venise
See Chapter 5, page 122. Quite the nearest to truly 'natural', and quite the lightest and most delicate of the Muscat dessert wines of France. The only one I know of, too, that is easily obtainable in Britain: Yapp Brothers of Mere, Wiltshire, ship more than one example.

Muscat de Frontignan
See Frontignan, above.

Muscat de Lunel
From east of Montpellier (Frontignan is to the west) and inland, not on the coast. But much of a muchness with the other Muscats.

Muscat de Mireval
The same applies to this, from very near Frontignan.

Muscat de Rivesaltes
And to this, from the hills north of Perpignan.

Muscat de Saint-Jean-de-Minervois
This comes from a small enclave of Muscat-grape-growing in
the wild mountain country east of Carcassonne, which otherwise is known principally as an area of the modest V D Q S wines
referred to in Chapter 7.

Rivesaltes
Rivesaltes Rancio
Mostly white Muscat wines, from north of Perpignan. For
Rancio see others, above.

Rasteau
Rasteau Rancio
From the southern Rhône valley, east of Orange, not far from
Beaumes de Venise, but not in the same class.

Vin de Frontignan
See Frontignan, above.

VINS DE LIQUEUR

Clairette du Languedoc
From the high, hilly country of Hérault, north-west of
Montpellier – better-known for rather ordinary white table
wine: see Chapter 7.

Côtes d'Agly
Côtes du Haut-Roussillon
See under Vins Doux Naturels, page 191.

Frontignan
Muscat de Frontignan
Vin de Frontignan
More powerful versions of the various V D N Frontignan wines
listed above.

Pineau des Charentes or Pineau Charentais
Sweet and strong, and the only VDL to have an *appellation* all
its own (Ratafia de Champagne is similar but has no *appellation*).

Made in the delimited Cognac area, from the fresh juice of
the grapes, red or white, of the region, the fermentation
checked, and the resultant liquor fortified, only by the brandy
of the region.

Cognac of the previous year is used, one part cognac to
two parts grape juice. It does not smell so nice as it tastes: it
is about as sweet and as strong as port, and drunk in the same
(French) way by the Cognaçais – as a sweet, strong apéritif,
served very cold.

The best *pineaux* are given a period of maturation in cask,
which the law does not require, but quality does.

Not my favourite drink – too sweet and too bland – but a
finger of *pineau* in a tall champagne tulip, topped up with
ice-cold fizz, makes a tolerable tipple.

French Wine Production, 1972, 1973, 1974, 1975, 1976

Quantities in hectolitres*

	1972	1973	1974	1975	1976
Total production	58,498,409	82,425,164	75,481,971	65,975,000	73,035,000
AOC Wines	10,037,361	13,634,407	11,767,285	10,169,000	13,019,000
VDQS Wines	3,134,045	3,614,190	2,636,793	2,820,000	2,894,000
Wines for distillation into cognac	6,295,049	10,707,423	7,713,873	9,942,000	9,048,000
Vins du pays, wines for blending, vermouth, etc.	39,031,954	54,469,144	53,363,820	43,044,000	48,073,000

The 1973 vintage was certainly the biggest since the nineteen-thirties, perhaps since the phylloxera plague; statistics were arrived at by different methods before the war.

*1 hectolitre = 100 litres.

Index of Principal Wines

MORE ABOUT PENGUINS
AND PELICANS

Penguinews, which appears every month, contains details of all the new books issued by Penguins as they are published. From time to time it is supplemented by *Penguins in Print*, which is our complete list of almost 5,000 titles.

A specimen copy of *Penguinews* will be sent to you free on request. Please write to Dept EP, Penguin Books Ltd, Harmondsworth, Middlesex, for your copy.

In the U.S.A.: For a complete list of books available from Penguins in the United States write to Dept CS, Penguin Books, 625 Madison Avenue, New York, New York 10022.

In Canada: For a complete list of books available from Penguins in Canada write to Penguin Books Canada Ltd, 2801 John Street, Markham, Ontario L3R 1B4.